Apr 5th, 2010

Rebecca

Happy 18th ......

May this be of some assistance
to you in difficult times. Seek
Peace of mind & happiness always.
Stay Strong.

Love
Mom

The Power of Prayer

God can sometimes seem kind of far away, can't he? At times, you might feel like he doesn't even know what's going on in your life and all of the hard things you're going through. But just imagine if you had a direct channel to the creator of the universe. Imagine if you could speak—or think—and he would hear you. More than that, he would *listen* to you. What would you say? That answer, whatever it is, is what makes up prayer.

Aside from reading God's message to us, there may be no greater opportunity for spiritual growth than talking directly to God through prayer. Just imagine: You have the chance to tell him your problems and fears and worries—as well as your praises and dreams and appreciation. It's evidence of his great love for his children that he accepts all of what we tell him—and actively responds to it.

Our approaching God in prayer is also proof of our faith. After all, you don't talk to someone who isn't there! And the really cool part is that the more we talk, the more we realize that God works in us through those conversations. He uses our own prayers to draw us closer to him, to help us see him more clearly.

This book of daily prayers has been specifically designed as a tool for those who talk to God. It includes prayers—both formal and informal, classic and modern—on lots of subjects. Some days have prayers of thanksgiving; other days offer requests for God's guidance; and still others lead the reader in prayers of praise to God for his grace, mercy, or creative genius.

Don't feel like you have to be limited by the prayers in this book. None of these prayers is any more acceptable or special than any other sincere communication from one of God's children. They are just offered as a starting place. Each can be prayed word-for-word or used as a blueprint for your own more specific prayer. Don't be afraid to add your own thoughts to a prayer. Remember—this is your chance to talk with God and tell him what's on your mind.

Additionally, at the end of each month you'll find a blank page for your own reflections. These spaces are set aside for you to write your own prayers, specific requests, items of praise and thanks, or notes about what God is teaching you through prayer and his word.

Whatever way you use the book, though, keep in mind that the chance to talk with God every day is an awesome privilege. Take full advantage of this beautiful gift from the Lord. Enjoy the book, and enjoy your special time with God!

I can do everything through him who gives me strength.
Philippians 4:13, NIV

Dear God,

It's another new year, and I want this one to be the greatest ever. I want to live right and honor you in school and in sports and with my friends. I want to quit doing those things that have been getting in the way of our relationship. This year, I want to be the person you made me to be.

The problem is that I feel this way every January 1. That nice, clean slate makes it seem like I can do anything. Then, after about three days, I'm right back to the same old me.

I know that you can truly change me and make me new if I remember to allow you to do it. This year, I really do want to change, and I want you to help me do it. Let me be open to you like never before.

One of the most attractive, magnetic characteristics of the Christ is His consistency. When you need Him, He is there. He's there even when you don't think you need Him! You're never too early or too late. He's never in a lousy mood nor will he ask you to call back during office hours.... With Him, there's no new year or old year.

—Charles Swindoll, Growing Strong in the Seasons of Life

January 2

Forget the former things; do not dwell on the past. See, I am doing a new thing! Now it springs up; do you not perceive it? I am making a way in the desert and streams in the wasteland.
Isaiah 43:18–19, NIV

Jesus,

It's hard to put the past behind me, even with this fresh start of a new year. There are some pretty ugly things back there that are hard to forget. But I know it's impossible to move ahead without first letting go of what's behind.

So, God, help me to let go. Open my eyes to see where you are leading me. I want to be refreshed and see the desert parts of my life filled with streams of cool water.

I am so glad you want to do this for me. If anyone knew just how I feel on the inside, some of the bad stuff that I am hiding, they would never believe it. But you know. And you still love me. And now you want to change me from a dusty, dry wasteland into a healthy landscape.

How can I thank you? I love you. Amen.

The driest desert can become the most lush garden if it is put into God's caring hands.

> **How great is the love the Father has
> lavished on us, that we should be called
> children of God! And that is what we are!**
> *1 John 3:1, NIV*

Father,

Father. I like to call you that. But it's a hard idea for me to understand. I have a human father. I love him, but he's not perfect. You're the ultimate Father of all time.

I know you didn't have to make us your children. You could have saved us and just made us your servants. Or your really good friends. Or your angels. But you took our relationship to the deepest level by making us your children—just like Jesus.

I don't get it, Father, but I like it. Thanks for making me part of your family. I like knowing I'm loved by you.

January 4

I call on you, O God, for you will answer me;
give ear to me and hear my prayer.

Psalm 17:6, NIV

I asked God for strength, that I might achieve.
I was made weak, that I might learn humbly to obey.

I asked for health, that I might do greater things.
I was given infirmity, that I might do better things.

I asked for riches, that I might be happy.
I was given poverty, that I might be wise.

I asked for power, that I might have the praise of men.
I was given weakness, that I might feel the need of God.

I asked for all things, that I might enjoy life.
I was given life, that I might enjoy all things.

I got nothing that I asked for—but everything I
        had hoped for.
Almost despite myself, my unspoken prayers were
        answered.

I am among all men most richly blessed.

—*unknown Confederate soldier*

God wants you to ask him for your heart's desires—but he
won't always answer your prayers. Instead, he promises to
always give you what you really need.

Keep on praying.
1 Thessalonians 5:17, NLT

Father,

Thank you for setting up this way for us to communicate. What a gift prayer is! I can actually talk to the God who created me. I can open my mouth or even just think of a prayer to you—and you actually hear me and respond. If I didn't know it was true, I wouldn't think it was possible.

Help me, Father, not to take prayer for granted. Help me to want to talk to you all the time—when I wake up, before I go to sleep, at school, at work, at home. I don't just want to talk to you when I need help or before a meal. I want to keep that line open 24/7. Thanks for always listening.

Work as if you were to live a hundred years. Pray as if you were to die tomorrow.

—Benjamin Franklin

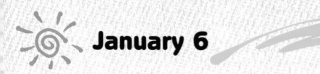

> **Friends, this world is not your home, so don't
> make yourselves cozy in it. Don't indulge your
> ego at the expense of your soul.**
> *1 Peter 2:11, TM*

God,

I believe that somewhere there's a heaven. I'm not sure what it looks like, where it is, or what life is like there, but I'm sure that people who love and follow you are there.

In the meantime, I live here, in the world that you created. And I *like* it here. I like my friends. I'm looking forward to a career and a family. I want to travel and see new places. I want to enjoy and appreciate the world around me without selling myself out to it. I want to look at your awesome creation, and I want to build strong relationships with the people in it.

But I don't want to adopt everything about this world. I don't want to be restricted by its ideas of success and image. Help me enjoy this world without becoming a captive in it, because I know I won't be here forever. Amen.

*The greatest, most wonderful, most
phenomenal thing on this earth won't be as
amazing as a single grain of sand in heaven.*

Many are asking, "Who can show us any good?"
Let the light of your face shine upon us, O Lord.
Psalm 4:6, NIV

Lord, how can I endure this life
of sorrow, unless you strengthen me
with your mercy and grace? Do not
turn your face from me. Do not withdraw your consolation from me, lest
my soul becomes like a water-
less desert. Teach me, O Lord,
to do your will, and to live
humbly. You alone know me perfectly, seeing into my soul. You
alone can give lasting peace and joy.

—*Thomas à Kempis*

*God's love for us is no secret. It's written all over
his face.*

January 8

Never pay back evil for evil to anyone. Do things in such a way that everyone can see you are honorable. Do your part to live in peace with everyone, as much as possible.
Romans 12:17–18, NLT

God,

You know I can get caught up in "justice" and making sure everything is right—especially for myself. I hate being taken advantage of. I don't want anyone to get away with treating me badly and taking what's mine or winning when they don't deserve to. And that attitude leads me to confrontations with people.

Sometimes that's good, God. Sometimes those people need to be confronted and straightened out. But I also know that, in the name of justice, I've caused some fights and hard feelings I didn't need to. I set out to make things right for me—not for you.

Help me, God, to know when to let things go—when not to fight. Help me to love peace as much as justice. Help me to let you make things right instead of trying to do it on my own.

I believe that for peace a man may, even should, do everything in his power. Nothing in this world could rank higher than peace.

—Anwar el-Sadat

**Give thanks in all circumstances, for this is
God's will for you in Christ Jesus.**
1 Thessalonians 5:18, NIV

Father,

Why is it so easy for me to forget to thank you for all
the cool things you do for me? I sure don't have trouble
remembering to ask you for stuff. I'm always right there in
your face when I've got a crisis. But when that crisis gets
settled, I never seem to get around to saying thanks.

Well, I want to tell you today that I *am* grateful for
everything you do for me. You've given me people in my
life who love me. You've come up with a way for us to
spend forever together. Most of all, I'm thankful that you're
always there for me—even when my life's not going all
that well.

Help me to remember to keep thanking you for everything you give me. Amen.

*Giving thanks to God is about more than just
being polite. It's an act of humility that
reminds me that all the good stuff is from
him—not from me.*

January 10

Jesus said, "You're blessed when you care.
At the moment of being 'care-full,' you find yourselves cared for."
Matthew 5:7, TM

Dear Father,
　　I know I dump a lot of stuff on you. But I love the fact that you really care about me—about my problems, my happiness, my everything. Thank you for caring about me. Thank you for caring about how I feel, for caring about my needs, for caring about my problems, and for caring about my day-to-day life. I can't even imagine how un-"care-full" life without you must feel.
　　I want to spread this feeling of care. Today, please show me someone that I can care for, whether it's just with a smile, a "Hey," a hug, or some words of encouragement. I want to learn more about noticing and caring for others so that they can feel your love and kindness through me.

It's not enough just to care about those who care about you. Try to care about everyone you see, meet, and know. Only then will you truly be living a "care-full" life.

All praise to the God and Father of our
Lord Jesus Christ. He is the source of every
mercy and the God who comforts us.
He comforts us in all our troubles so that we
can comfort others. When others are
troubled, we will be able to give them the
same comfort God has given us.
2 Corinthians 1:3–4, NLT

Dear God,

   I have a good friend who's hurting right now, and I'm
not sure what to say or do to help. I want to try to do
something, and that's why I'm talking to you. I know how
nice it is to have you to turn to when I'm feeling low.
You've comforted me so much in the past. Please do that
for my friend.

   And help me to know how to comfort or encourage or
just plain listen—whatever it will take to make a difference
for my friend. Help me to know the right thing to say or do.
We both really need your help right now.

*Who's more qualified to encourage than someone who's been
encouraged? Who's better at comforting than someone who
has received comfort? Who better to love than one who's
been loved?*

The fool says in his heart, "There is no God."
Psalm 14:1, NIV

Father,

I believe in you—I do. But so many people don't believe in you. Some of them are really smart, and that makes me wonder. Does it make more sense to trust a God I can't see but am convinced of? Wouldn't it be smarter just to trust myself to run my life the best I can?

But then I think of how often I've turned to you in the bad times or when I've had a big decision to make. It's so nice to have you there with me. I guess you and I both know I've got a better chance with you in charge and helping me along. No, I can't prove to others that you're real, but all I have to do is look at all the changes you've made in my life and in other people's lives to know you're there.

I guess what I need is help to grow my faith.

Faith is a desperate dive out of the sinking boat of human effort and a prayer that God will be there to pull us out of the water.
—Max Lucado, The Gift for All People

You're blessed when you're content with just who you are—no more, no less. That's the moment you find yourselves proud owners of everything that can't be bought.
Matthew 5:5, TM

Dear God,

I know you created me just the way I am. But some-times—no, *lots* of times—I wish I were different. Smarter. More talented. Cuter. More popular. It's hard to be content with who I am when I feel like so many people are always telling me I should be better. Don't they know they make me feel like a loser?

But I know that with you on my side, I could never really be a loser, God. Help me to do the best I can, wherever I am, whatever I'm doing. But also help me to accept my weak-nesses gracefully. I don't want to waste my whole life trying to be someone I'm not. Thank you for making me just the way I am and for always loving the real me. Amen.

If God had wanted you to be someone else, he would have made you someone else. Celebrate your individuality for what it is—a present from God.

January 14

Work for the food that sticks with you, food that nourishes your
lasting life, food the Son of Man provides. He and what he does
are guaranteed by God the Father to last.

John 6:27, TM

We're hungry for something Lord.
We have so much rich food and cake and candy
        for ourselves, but we're hungry.
People around us are so stiff and tight and hard to reach.
And they make us that way.
But we're hungry for something more.
People we know keep talking about great ideas,
        brilliant questions, and the problem of God's
        existence.
But we're hungry for You, not ideas or theories.
We want You to touch us, to reach inside us and turn us on.
There are so many people who will counsel us to death.
But we're hungry for someone who really knows
        You and has You, someone who can get so close
        to us that we can see You there.
We have so many things, but we're hungry for You.
Deep, deep down inside we're hungry, even if we
        appear to be silly, lazy, or unconcerned at times.
We're hungry for Your kind of power and love and joy.
Feed us, Lord, feed us with Your rich food.

—Anonymous

January 15

> I keep asking that the God of our Lord Jesus Christ, the glorious Father, may give you the Spirit of wisdom and revelation, so that you may know him better.
>
> *Ephesians 1:17, NIV*

God,

I just can't get enough of you. We both know I don't always feel that way, but right now I want to know *everything*. I want to know what you're really like. I want to know what your plans are. I want to know if anything makes you laugh. I want to be with you and just hang out.

I know I can't really know you and be with you until I'm in heaven, but help me to know you as well as I possibly  can here on earth. Help me to keep discovering new little—or big—truths about you all the time. Help me to never get tired of talking to you and reading your words.

When you boil down all the great mysteries of the universe, the only real question is God. He is the mystery that answers them all. The more he is revealed, the more the puzzle is solved.

Jesus once again addressed them: "I am the world's Light. No one who follows me stumbles around in the darkness. I provide plenty of light to live in."
John 8:12, TM

Jesus,

A lot of my friends don't know you very well. Some of them don't even believe in you. I don't understand that at all because, to me, you are so real.

I wish I could make them believe. I see them really struggling with life, making bad decisions (which I admit I do, too, when I choose to ignore you). They always seem to be searching for something that will give their lives meaning. I want to shake them and say, "Don't you get it?! There's more to life!"

But I know I can't do that. It's their own choice. I hope they find you. In the meantime, God, help me love them the way you do, and help me live a life that reflects your light to them. Since that's all I can really do, I want to do it the best I can. Amen.

The best way to tell your friends about Jesus is not through words but through loving actions.

**In Christ's family there can be no
division into Jew and non-Jew, slave
and free, male and female.
Among us you are all equal.**
Galatians 3:28, TM

I see white and black, Lord.
I see white teeth in a black face.
I see black eyes in a white face.
Help me to see persons, Jesus—not a black person
or a white person, a red person or a yellow person,
but human persons.

—*Malcolm Boyd*, Are You Running With Me, Jesus?

*Red and yellow, black and white, they
are precious in his sight. Jesus loves
the little children of the world.*
—*Children's song*

January 18

> **Above all else, guard your heart, for it
> affects everything you do.**
> *Proverbs 4:23, NLT*

God,

You know how excited I am about my new love. I've never felt anything like this before. I know this is totally corny, but it's just like in the movies. I'm so happy. I can't quit thinking about our relationship. I can't quit smiling. I don't ever want it to end.

But even in the middle of all these great feelings, I need to stay focused on you. I know I'm in kind of a "danger zone." This person could ask me for almost anything, and I think I'd give it. Am I really ready for this kind of a relationship? I don't know. To be honest, it's hard for me to care right now. I just want to feel this way forever!

Please protect me, Lord. Please help me to be careful. Help me to honor you with everything I do or say. Help me not to get further into this than is healthy and right for me. Help me to care more about making you happy than I do about this other person. Help me to stay focused on you.

A new relationship is exciting, but try to go into every new situation prepared. When you haven't made up your mind about what is right ahead of time, your emotions can easily lead you in the wrong direction.

The one thing I want from God, the thing I seek most of all, is the privilege of meditating in his Temple, living in his presence every day of my life, delighting in his incomparable perfections and glory. There I'll be when troubles come. He will hide me.

Psalm 27:4–5, TLB

Dear God,

There are so many things that I'd like to have—good friends, some extra cash, a good future, an easy year at school—but when I actually say them out loud, they seem so insignificant. Sure, I'd *like* to have them, but do I really need them? Are those the things that are going to make me happy, content, fulfilled, or satisfied?

When I take the time to really think about it, I realize that the only thing I really need—and the only thing I *really* want—is you, God. I want to know you. I want to talk to you. I want to see you in the world around me. Please help me to live my entire life with you at the center.

Knowing the difference between what you want and what you need is a big step toward maturity. An even bigger step occurs when you are willing to give up what you want in order to get what you need.

January 20

God,

   Do you ever feel like you've been cheapened? Do you feel like people just look for and think about you when it's convenient and popular? Right now, "spiritual" is in style. My friends talk about angels and meditation and miracles. There are stories about "spirituality" in almost every magazine. But I don't think those people really know you—the true you, the living God.

   People are so used to being able to buy or get whatever they want or whatever is in fashion. Since "spirituality" is in fashion, it's being promoted everywhere, which seems like it would be a good thing. But it's a strange spirituality. It doesn't talk about deep issues, surrender, or life changes. It's like God Lite or god with a lowercase *g* or something. I want more than "god"—I want you, God. I want more than just being "spiritual"—I want a personal relationship with you. I want more than curiosity—I want commitment.

God is not a product, a passing fad, or a hobby. He is pure and everlasting, and he is the one true God.

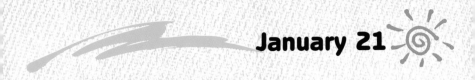

The human mind may devise many plans, but it is the purpose of the Lord that will be established.
Proverbs 19:21, NRSV

Father,

Some people lead such incredible lives for you. They witness for you all the time, or they make careers out of singing praise songs for you, or they travel the world telling people your story. My life just seems so ordinary compared to theirs. What can I give you?

I can just give you myself and all that I can do. I'm not sure yet what my gifts or skills are, but they're yours, God. I want you to know that I'm here and I'm available for whatever you want to do with me. My life doesn't have to be exciting, but I'd like it to mean something for you.

I wonder what God is doing with my life. Like my purpose. What does God have in store for me? Where do my talents and gifts lie? For now, I'll just take it day by day. I'm confident that I'll know someday. Maybe I'll look back at my life and think "Oh, so that was it!" Isn't it amazing, this plan we're part of?

—Cassie Bernall, victim of the Columbine High School massacre. Written in a letter to a friend less than a year before her death.

January 22

Remember your Creator in the days of your youth.
Ecclesiastes 12:1, NIV

Lord,
    Sometimes I forget how amazing you are. I get so busy with school and work and practice that I forget you're still here. You're still holding everything together. You're still loving and taking care of me. You're still God.
    I just want you to know that, right now, I'm remembering you. I'm remembering to be blown away again by the beauty of your creation. I'm remembering to be grateful for all of the cool people you've put in my life to love me. I'm remembering to be humbled by the sacrifice you made for me.
    Thank you, Father, for helping me to remember. Amen.

A lot of growing up has to do with learning which things to remember and which things to forget.

> God said, "My child, don't ignore it
> when the Lord disciplines you, and don't be
> discouraged when he corrects you. For the
> Lord disciplines those he loves, and he
> punishes those he accepts as his children."
> *Hebrews 12:5–6, NIV*

Lord,

I sometimes feel like I don't fit in anywhere, like I just don't belong. But it really matters to you whether I keep walking with you, doesn't it? When I read in the Bible that you've made me your child, I don't get the idea that you're just going to let me walk away from you.

One verse I read even says you discipline those you love. Honestly, the thought of being disciplined by you scares me. And you know I don't like being told what to do. But it makes me feel so taken care of to know you're willing to go to that trouble to keep us close and to keep me from wasting my life on things that don't please you.

Thank you for loving me that much.

January 24

Now to him who is able to keep you from falling,
and to make you stand without blemish in the
presence of his glory with rejoicing, to the only
God our Savior, through Jesus Christ our Lord, be
glory, majesty, power, and authority, before all
time and now and forever. Amen.

Jude 24, NRSV

God be in my head, and in my understanding;
God be in my eyes, and in my looking;
God be in my mouth, and in my speaking;
God be in my heart, and in my thinking;
God be at my end, and at my departing.

—Sarum Primer

*God is available at any place,
during any time, for any
circumstance, in any situation.
Always remember, the most
powerful being in the universe is
there for you 24/7.*

January 25

For I can do everything with the help of
Christ who gives me the strength I need.
Philippians 4:13, NLT

God,

    Some days, it's so obvious I need you. Everything I try on my own falls apart in my hands. I decide what I will do, and I just go. For some stupid reason, it doesn't occur to me to ask for your help. I assume if I want something, then I can just make it happen. Thanks for reminding me that I'm nothing without you.

    On the other hand, I love those days when I include you in all I do. It's not like everything goes perfectly. But I know you're there with me. I know I'm working in your strength—and anything you want to happen through me will happen. What a difference!

    Help me to live in your power on this day and every other day. I need you so much.

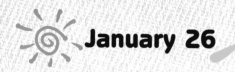

January 26

The Lord does not look at the things man looks at. Man looks at the outward appearance, but the Lord looks at the heart.

1 Samuel 16:7, NIV

God,

Do you have any idea how much I want other people to think I look good? There, I said it. Sometimes I just feel ugly, and everything on TV and in magazines makes it seem like I'm just naturally supposed to look great all the time. What's that about?

God, please help me to be satisfied with how I look and please help me not to worry about it so much. Help me to feel good about myself no matter what I look like. I don't want to spend the rest of my life thinking about this.

Help me to care more about what you think of me than what other people do (including myself!).

Often, beauty, as the world defines it, is not a blessing. Incredible as it may seem, sometimes beauty is the beast that drives a girl to depression or robs a boy of his self-esteem. There are many "beautiful" people who happen to be lonely, insecure, and unfulfilled.

—Josh McDowell and Bob Hostetler, Don't Check Your Brains at the Door

I've decided, Lord, that I don't like fights.
I have a friend who is mad at me,
and we're each waiting for the other to apologize. . . .

Something tells me, Lord, that isn't going to happen.
So I'm asking you for some help.
Give me the willingness to take the first step
toward making this right.
Help me not to put this off too long.
I know that letting a fight go on
can lead to resentment, bitterness, and even hatred.

This is my friend, Lord.
How could I forget that?
I really do want to get back on track
with this valuable person in my life.
So, Lord, turn us both around
to face you and
to face each other.

You're a master when it comes to forgiveness.
I suppose that's why I came to you. Amen.

—*Dean Nadasdy*, Tough Days and Talks with God

How many friendships have ended because neither person was strong enough to apologize after a fight?

Father God,
Why is it that I think I must get somewhere, assume some
position, be gathered together, or separated apart in
the quiet of my study to pray?
Why is it that I feel that I have to go somewhere or do some
particular act to find you, reach you, and talk
with you?
Your presence is here
In the city—on the busy bus, in the factory, in the
cockpit of the airplane; in the hospital—in the
patients' rooms, in the intensive care unit, in the
waiting room; in the home—at dinner, in the
bedroom, in the family room, at my workbench;
in the car—in the parking lot, at the stoplight.
Lord, reveal your presence to me everywhere, and help me
become aware of your presence each moment of
the day.
May your presence fill the nonanswers, empty glances, and
lonely times of my life. Amen.

—*Robert Wood*, A Thirty-Day Experiment in Prayer

**God is here, there . . . everywhere. Look for him around you—and
you will find him.**

> **Barnabas and Paul cried out, "We don't make God; he makes us, and all of this— sky, earth, sea, and everything in them."**
>
> *Acts 14:15, TM*

Dear God,

Sometimes I find myself thinking about you in different ways. If I'm feeling lonely, I think about you as my friend. If I'm scared, I think of you as my comforter. If I'm worried, I think about you as my source of peace. If I'm angry, I think of you as my sounding board. If I'm happy, I think about you as my loving father.

I can't tell you how cool I think it is that you can be all of these things to me. But is it wrong that I always limit you to just one role or the other?

I don't want to give you just one role in my life. I don't want to think about you in just the way that's most convenient to me. I don't want to cram you into some mold that only suits my purposes.

God, I want to know all of you and to understand how huge and magnificent you are. I never want to make the mistake of imagining you are smaller than you really are. Help me to realize that you can always be all things to me—not just one thing or another. Amen.

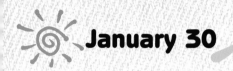

So you should not be like cowering, fearful slaves. You should behave instead like God's very own children, adopted into his family—calling him "Father, dear Father." For his Holy Spirit speaks to us deep in our hearts and tells us that we are God's children.
Romans 8:15–16, NLT

God,

So much of my identity is wrapped up in my parents. They so often define who I am. I'm not really sure how I feel about that. I don't totally mind, but I'm ready to be seen as my own unique individual, not just as my parents' kid.

But with you, I don't want to pull away as I get older. I want to come *closer*. Long after I stop relying on my mom as my main source of advice and companionship, I'll be going to you, saying, "What's next?"

The great part is that I know I'll always be able to trust your answer to that question. You are a perfect Father. And I can't thank you enough for that. Amen.

As your Father, God is always waiting for you to jump into his lap and put your arms around his neck so he can whisper, "I love you, child" in your ear.

Dear God,

I've done it again. I took control of my life and tried to lead it in the direction I thought was best. I didn't mean to leave you out of things, but it happened anyway. I'm sorry. It's hard to remember that when I let you do the leading, that's when I really experience life.

Sometimes I forget that you are God—the one who made me and knows me best—and instead I act like *I'm* God, trying to run the whole show and be the leader.

I wish you'd just push me out of the way and get things back on track, but you're not like that. You just wait patiently for me to figure it out—again. Well, here I am, ready to let you set the pace.

Don't give up on following Christ just because you fall down. There's no such thing as a Christian who never stumbles. Real Christians are the ones who get up and go on.

—Kevin Johnson,
What Do Ya Know?

My Thoughts & Prayers

What's been on your mind (and heart) this month? Have you had any big answers to prayer? What's your most important prayer request? Use this space to keep track of all that's been going on.

_____

_____

_____

_____

_____

_____

_____

_____

_____

_____

_____

_____

_____

_____

_____

_____

February 1

You will show me the way of life, granting me the joy of your presence and the pleasures of living with you forever.
Psalm 16:11, NLT

Loving God, who sees in us nothing that you have not given yourself, make my body healthy and agile, my mind sharp and clear, my heart joyful and contented, my soul faithful and loving. And surround me with the company of men and angels who share my devotion to you.

Above all let me live in your presence, for with you all fear is banished, and there is only harmony and peace. Let every day combine the beauty of spring, the brightness of summer, the abundance of autumn, and the repose of winter. And at the end of my life on earth, grant that I may come to see and know you in the fullness of your glory.

—*Thomas Aquinas*

The gift of life is sweeter when we remember who gave it to us.

February 2

Do not forsake me, O Lord; O my God,
do not be far from me;
make haste to help me, O Lord,
my salvation.

Psalm 38:21–22, NRSV

God,

Don't abandon me. My life is so hard right now. I pray, but I don't feel like you're hearing me. I try to think about you, but I don't feel like you're really there.

I'm depressed, God. Things seem dark and uncertain. Why do I sometimes feel like this? I can't explain it. Nothing has really changed. It's just that right now, it seems like it's all more than I can handle.

God, I feel so lost and afraid. I need you so much. I'm sorry for doubting that you're here for me. I'm just so scared. Please help me to know that I can always rely on you and your love.

In your darkest moments, when God is the most difficult to see, maybe it's because he is standing underneath you, holding you up.

God,

The hardest place for me to feel your presence is at school—and that's the place where I think I need to feel you the most. It's so hard to be surrounded by some of the attitudes, some of the habits, and some of the actions of the kids there. You say you're near me all the time—but how can I experience that at school when I see all sorts of bad stuff around me?

OK, so on one level, I know that you're there with me, helping me to get through each day. But it can be easy to forget that. Help me not to become discouraged and think that you're far away and out of touch with what's going on. Help me to realize that you're always with me—not waiting outside or hiding around a corner, but right there with me.

I just need to figure out how to stay in touch with you while I'm at school. Teach me how to be with you all day long. Amen.

One of the greatest things about prayer is you don't need any tools outside of yourself to do it. Prayer brings you closer to God, and you can pray anywhere, anytime.

> If you need wisdom—if you want to know what
> God wants you to do—ask him, and he will gladly
> tell you. He will not resent you asking.
>
> *James 1:5, NLT*

Dear Lord,

Thinking about all the decisions I'm going to have to make in the next few years really blows my mind. They all seem like such really *big*, important ones. What classes am I going to take? What clubs or sports should I try out for? How many hours should I work a week? What college should I go to? Do I even want to go to college?

God, I could really use your wisdom here. I can't make all these decisions on my own. I'm sure I'm going to mess something up. Please help me to make the best choices I possibly can.

Thanks for promising to give me your wisdom when I ask for it.

Wisdom isn't a collection of facts like most people think. Wisdom is actually knowing what to do with the facts once you've got them.

**The prayer of a righteous person has great
power and wonderful results.**
James 5:16, NLT

Father,

    I pray all these prayers. I spend all this time talking to you. But sometimes I can't stop myself from wondering if you're really there and if you can hear me. Is any of this praying making a difference? Am I just talking to myself? You know I wrestle with these doubts, God.

    But then I remember—and I do believe you're the one who reminds me—all of the prayers you've answered, all of the different ways you've responded to me through my life and through the Bible. It seems crazy that the God of the universe would care what I have to say and respond to it. But I believe it, God. I really do. Thank you for hearing and answering my prayers. Thank you that they do make a difference.

*More things are wrought by prayer
than this world dreams of.*
—Alfred, Lord Tennyson

February 6

> But the time is coming and is already here when true worshipers will worship the Father in spirit and in truth. The Father is looking for anyone who will worship him that way.
>
> *John 4:23, NLT*

God,

I know you are great. In fact, you're so great and so big that sometimes it paralyzes me. What can I say to you that could come anywhere close to describing your greatness? How could any words I dream up begin to capture the depth of your love? It almost feels pointless to try to worship you because I have so little to offer you.

But I must worship you. It's the only response I can give to your magnificence—and it's what I was made to do. Help me, Father, to know how to respond to your greatness. Help me to worship you in the best way any human can. Help me to worship you with my words, with my thoughts, with my life. Amen.

It is only when men begin to worship
that they begin to grow.
—Calvin Coolidge

For we are what he has made us, created in
Christ Jesus for good works, which God prepared
beforehand to be our way of life.

Ephesians 2:10, NRSV

Christ has
No body now on earth but yours;
No hands but yours;
No feet but yours;
Yours are the eyes
Through which is to look out
Christ's compassion to the world;
Yours are the feet
With which he is to go about
Doing good;
Yours are the hands
With which he is to bless now.

—St. Teresa of Ávila

*Part of your job as a child of God is to let other people see
Christ reflected in the way you act, the way you speak, the
way you think, and the way you love others. You are his
instrument of goodness.*

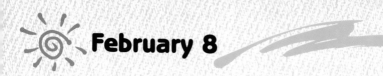
Don't let anyone look down on you because you are young, but set an example for the believers in speech, in life, in love, in faith and in purity.
1 Timothy 4:12, NIV

Dear God,

    I get so tired of people thinking I can't do some things just because I'm young. Yes, I'm young. But that's not a bad thing! Because of it, I'm strong and energetic and ready to do new things. In fact, I think I can do lots of things older people can't—or won't. Most important, I've got you. And with you, I can do anything, right?

    So help me to live strong and hard for you right now, Father. Help me to use my youth to bring glory to you and do great things for you. Work through me to bring others closer to you and to make a difference in your world. Please, Lord, help others to see you in me.

Young people will respond if the challenge is tough enough and hard enough.... Young people were built for God, and without God as the center of their lives, they become frustrated and confused, desperately grasping for and searching for security.
—Billy Graham

**Blessed are you who give yourselves over to God,
turn your backs on the world's "sure thing," ignore
what the world worships.**

Psalm 40:4, TM

God,

When people find out I'm a Christian, they often say things to me like they could never follow God because it would mean giving up everything. I don't think that's true at all. You've never asked me to give up everything. You've only asked me to follow your truth. When I do that, God, there are some things that I give up on my own. I give up the lie that says my value comes from my appearance or my talent or my intelligence. I give up the desire to own everything I see. I give up the idea that some people are more important than other people, simply because of how they talk or the color of their skin or what country they're from.

God, the things I've given up are all worthless. I can't believe I spent so much of my life hanging on to them. And everything I've gained through you is so *worthy*! Thank you for showing me another way to live and to love.

Giving yourself to God doesn't mean you have to give up on the world. It means you're finally free to give up on some of the world's ideas.

February 10

Jesus said, Love the Lord your God with all your passion and prayer and intelligence. This is the most important, the first on any list. But there is a second to set alongside it: Love others as well as you love yourself. These two commands are pegs; everything in God's Law and the Prophets hangs from them.
Matthew 22:37–40, TM

God,

This is the month where everyone thinks and talks a lot about love. It's easy to love you. You're awesome. You're loving. You're compassionate. You created a totally cool world.

And it's easy to love certain people. My friends. My family (well, most of the time). You know, the people in my life that I trust the most.

But everyone else? I'm really supposed to love everyone else as much as I love myself? That seems impossible. I think I'm going to need your help—and lots of it.

At least it's nice to know that following you isn't really that complicated. It's just about loving you and loving other people. That seems more manageable than having a bunch of guidelines and rules and lists. God, I do love you. Deeply. Help me transfer that love to other people. Amen.

When in doubt about what to say, do, or think, simply ask yourself: Does it show love for God and love for others? That is the only guideline you'll ever need.

> Jesus said, "Can all your worries add a single
> moment to your life? Of course not."
> *Matthew 6:27, NLT*

Lord,
    You know how stressed out I get about life. I worry about everything I've got to get done. I worry about what will happen if I don't get it done. I worry about the fact that I'm not getting things done while I'm worrying. I worry that I worry too much. I worry that I'm not worrying enough about the right things. All this worrying makes me *crazy!*
    Father, I want to get off this merry-go-round of worry. I want to really trust you with the things I can't control—and even the things I can control. I want to give it all to you and let it go. Why, Father, is it so hard for me to do that? I don't get it. Please help me to trust you more and to worry less.

Worry does not empty tomorrow of its sorrow; it empties today of its strength.
                —Corrie ten Boom

February 12

There is a time for everything, and a season for every activity under heaven: . . . a time to be silent and a time to speak.
Ecclesiastes 3:1, 7, NIV

Give unto us, O Lord, that quietness of mind in which we can hear you speaking to us, for your own name's sake.

Lord, you have taught us in your word that there is a
    time to speak and a time to keep silence.
As we thank you for the power of speech,
    we pray for the grace of silence.
Make us as ready to listen as we are to talk,
    ready to listen to your voice in the quietness
    of our hearts
and ready to listen to other people who need a
    sympathetic ear.
Show us when to open our mouths and when to hold
    our peace
that we may glorify you both in speech and silence
    through Jesus Christ our Lord.
                    —*Frank Colquhoun*

The ability to remain silent—and be at peace in the silence—is as important as the ability to say the right thing at the right time.

Above all else, guard your heart,
for it is the wellspring of life.
Proverbs 4:23, NIV

Dear God,

It's almost Valentine's Day, God, and all I can think about is how I really want to be in love. I'm so sick of being "just friends." I want someone I can spend all of my time thinking about and hanging out with. I want someone who will care about me more than anyone else in the world. I want it so much, it's scary.

Help me to be careful not to jump into a relationship with the wrong person just so I can be with someone. Help me to wait for the right person and the right time. Help me to care more about my relationship with you than my relationship with anyone else in the world.

Learning to love—and
to be loved by—God is
the best preparation
for any relationship.

February 14

Love is patient; love is kind; love is not envious or boastful or arrogant or rude. It does not insist on its own way; it is not irritable or resentful; it does not rejoice in wrongdoing, but rejoices in the truth. It bears all things, believes all things, hopes all things, endures all things.
1 Corinthians 13:4–8, NRSV

Lord,

You know where my love life stands right now. But today, on Valentine's Day, I want you to know that I love you more than any other person in my life. How could I not after the way you've loved me? You gave your life for me. You set me free from myself. You're preparing a home for me with you in heaven.

Thank you for loving me the way you do. Thank you for giving me the ability to love you back. Help me to know how to put that love into action—even when the emotions come and go. Help my love for you to be even stronger when the next Valentine's Day rolls around. Amen.

God's way of putting people right shows up in the acts of faith, confirming what Scripture has said all along: "The person in right standing before God by trusting him really lives."

Romans 1:17, TM

Father,

I have a few friends who think I'm crazy for believing in you. They think Christians live boring lives. They think we're a group of empty-headed robots. They think Christians will never really learn how to live.

How can I tell them that it's just the opposite? That being a Christian is all about learning how to really live?

With you in my life, I'm free from so many things. It's cool not to have to worry about proving my worth to everyone else. I don't have to wear a mask to get other people's approval. I don't have to worry about being alone. I don't have to worry about being unloved.

You give my life structure and meaning. I actually feel more free with you than without you—free to live the way I was *meant* to. Thank you for giving me that chance. Amen.

True freedom is found only within the boundaries of a loving relationship with God.

February 16

I feel like singing this morning, O Lord.
I feel like telling everyone about me
     how great you are.
If only they could know the depths of your love
     and your eternal concern for those who will follow you!
But my songs are so often off-key.
My speech is so inadequate.
I simply cannot express what I feel,
     what I know to be true about your love
        for your creatures upon this world.

But even the songs of the birds
     proclaim your praises.
The heavens and the earth beneath them
     the trees that reach toward you,
     the flowers that glow in colorful beauty,
     the green hills and soaring mountains,
     the valleys and the plains,
     the lakes and the rivers,
     the great oceans that pound our shores,
     they proclaim your greatness, O God,
     and your love for the sons of men.

How glorious it is to be alive, O Lord!
May every breath of my body,
     every beat of my heart,
     be dedicated to your praise and glory.
          —Leslie Brandt

> He who trusts in himself is a
> fool, but he who walks in
> wisdom is kept safe.
> *Proverbs 28:26, NIV*

God,
 Sometimes, it's hard for me to admit when I'm wrong. OK, it's hard to do that all the time. I don't know why I can't just be objective and see that I've said or done something wrong, admit it, and move on. For some reason, I'm kind of blind to my own problems.
 Help me, God, to be honest with myself about everything. Help me not to lie to myself because I want to believe that I'm better than I am. I can't deal with my problems if I can't admit them. Please give me the sight to see both my strengths and my weaknesses—and the courage to keep growing in you.

*The greatest of faults, I should
say, is to be conscious of none.*
—*Thomas Carlyle*

February 18

You know, God, so many kids want to be popular—part of the cool crowd. I'm not in that crowd, but I'm not really unpopular either. I sort of enjoy being somewhere in the middle of that scale.

I don't have to look cool or say cool things. I hang with my friends, have lots of fun doing stuff with my family, and can live with myself at the end of the day. I don't have to worry about what everyone thinks of me. It's a breeze to get ready for school—who would notice if I don't have the newest sneakers? As far as I can tell, everyone likes me. No pressure there!

Maybe someday I'll be a shining star, but for right now, I'm free to be me. Now *that's* cool.

With popularity comes a lot of stress to hold on to that status. The most glorious freedom of all can be the freedom to just be yourself—without pressure, without expectations, without fear.

February 19

**You're blessed when you can show people how
to cooperate instead of compete or fight.**

Matthew 5:9, TM

Dear Lord,

There is so much competition in the world around me that I can't stand it. Everyone seems to be trying to get one step ahead of everyone else, no matter how many people might get stepped on or hurt in the process. It seems like people's talk about love, respect, and kindness is just that—all talk. The real message is "Get ahead," "Me first," and "Look out for number one."

I find myself falling into that trap too often, trying to be the focus of attention so that I won't be forgotten or ignored by the crowd. But God, I'd really like to be a person who does the opposite, who looks out for others instead of thinking only of myself. Please help me with that. Amen.

If you focus too much on pushing ahead, you may look up to find that you're all alone and you've left some great people behind. Look around you, think of others, and encourage everyone to move forward together.

Jesus said, "Come to me, all you that are weary and are carrying heavy burdens, and I will give you rest. Take my yoke upon you, and learn from me; for I am gentle and humble in heart, and you will find rest for your souls. For my yoke is easy, and my burden is light."

Matthew 11:28–30, NRSV

God,

What I want more than anything is:

- to be with you.
- to get away from it all.
- to take a real rest and be refreshed.
- to live freely.
- to walk lightly.

Can you do that for me? Even in the midst of my busy, crazy, out-of-control life? I want that so much. I'll keep trying to learn as long as you keep teaching me.

With God, you can get away from it all without ever actually going anywhere.

My health may fail, and my spirit may grow weak, but God remains the strength of my heart; he is mine forever.
Psalm 73:26, NLT

God, it's hard to have self-confidence when things aren't going the way I want or the way I think they should. If I'm doing badly in school, if my friends and I aren't getting along, if everything I do seems to turn sour, if I'm feeling depressed or down... well, God, I just want to curl up and disappear. I feel like a failure.

I guess if I spend my whole life depending on myself and how well I do things, I'll always be disappointed. But if I spend my life depending on you, then my self-confidence will be there. It's all in how I look at things, so please give me the right perspective. Thanks.

The best way to have self-confidence
is to stop focusing on yourself.

February 22

Jesus said, "I no longer call you servants, because a servant does not know his master's business. Instead, I have called you friends, for everything that I learned from my Father I have made known to you."

John 15:15, NIV

When the sins in my soul are increasing, I lose the taste for virtuous things. Yet even at such moments, Lord, I know I am failing you—and failing myself. You alone can restore my taste for virtue. There are so many false friends willing to encourage sin. But your friendship alone can give the strength of mind to resist and defeat sin.

—*St. Teresa of Ávila*

Our friendships make or break us. Who better to have as a friend than Jesus?

February 23

**Doing, not hearing, is what makes
the difference with God.**
Romans 2:13, TM

God,
   I've heard and learned a lot of things about you over the years. Most of it makes sense to me. But there are some things, God, that seem impossible for me to do, like loving people who don't exactly like me or treat me well. I know you want me to love them, and I know it's the right thing to do, but it is *so* hard. It's easiest for me just to ignore or avoid people who I know don't like me. But to actually *love* them? If you weren't God, I'd say, "You must be kidding."
   Why isn't it enough for me to just stay out of their way, to not bother them and to not hate them back? I can handle the "don't hate" part. It's the "love" part that trips me up.
   This is a tough one, God, and I'm especially going to need your help. I know you want me to live out what I've learned from you, so please give me the strength to learn to love people who hate me. Amen.

February 24

> And even we Christians ... groan to be released from pain and suffering. We, too, wait anxiously for that day when God will give us our full rights as his children, including the new bodies he promised us. Now that we are saved, we eagerly look forward to this freedom.
>
> *Romans 8:23–24, NLT*

God,

Heaven sounds so amazing, and if I think about it too much, I want to be there with you right away. I've caught the idea that heaven is my home, and I know I belong with you. I know now that I'm not going to be completely free, completely satisfied, completely "arrived" until I'm with you in heaven forever.

Life here on earth can get pretty hard to bear some-times, and the peace and beauty of heaven sounds so tempting. During these hard times, please comfort me through your word and my family and friends. God, until the day you call me home, please give me the patience to keep hoping in you, to keep looking forward to my home with you. Thank you that I will be with you someday. Thank you that I do have a hope and a future. Thank you that you will always love me and that you will bring me home when it's time.

Patience is the art of hoping.
—Vauvernargues

> Praise the Lord, O my soul. I will praise the Lord all
> my life; I will sing praise to my God as long as I live.
>
> *Psalm 146:1–2, NIV*

God,

I've been thinking about what was going on the day you created the universe. Take the color blue, for instance. When you made that color, you were really on a roll. The blue sky, the color of the lake, the color of my friend's eyes, the blueberries in my Wheaties. All of that beauty amazes me!

I wish I could do something that creative—come up with something as awesome as the color blue. But lots of things are totally in your hands. Thanks for coming up with blue . . . and red and yellow and green. Every time I see a rainbow, I'm going to think of you with a giant paint palette, coloring our world.

If I keep my eyes on God, I won't trip over my own feet.
Psalm 25:15, TM

God,
    I have so many goals for myself. I want to do well in school. I want to decide on a career that I'll truly enjoy. I'd like to live a good life. (I don't want to be rich—just able to live comfortably.) I think I'd like to be married and have a family someday so I can share my life with them. I want to work at staying physically fit and healthy. I want to find some way that I can help other people.
    Those goals are all good—I think you'd approve. But most important of all, I want to keep you first in my life. I want you to lead me. I want to learn more about you. I want to get closer and closer to you.
    As long as that goal remains first, I think the rest will fall into place. God, you are everything to me. I forget to tell you that sometimes, but it's true.

The best way to reach a goal is to keep it clearly in your sight.

February 27

To watch over mouth and tongue
is to keep out of trouble.
Proverbs 21:23, NRSV

Father,
   It's not true what they say—that words can't hurt me.
Words hurt terribly. Being called names or being talked
about makes me feel terrible.
   I have to admit that sometimes I do the same thing to
other people. I know I should watch what I say and think
before I speak. But sometimes the words just seem to spill
out of my mouth. And as soon as they do, I regret it. The
worst part is that once something's been said, there's no
way to take it back. Even if I apologize, I know the damage
has already been done. Unfortunately, "I'm sorry" can't
make everything OK.
   God, I don't want to be a gossip. I don't want to be the
kind of person who's always looking for something juicy to
talk about. I want to be a person whose words are kind and
encouraging, not mean and destructive. Please help me be
that person. Amen.

*Sticks and stones may break some bones,
but words can break a heart.*

**God opposes the proud but gives
grace to the humble.**
James 4:6, NIV

O God of earth and altar,
Bow down and hear our cry,
Our earthly rulers falter,
Our people drift and die;
The walls of gold entomb us,
The swords of scorn divide,
Take not your thunder from us,
But take away our pride!
From all that terror teaches,
From lies of tongue and pen,
From all the easy speeches,
That comfort cruel men,
From sale and profanation
Of honor and the sword,
From sleep and from
      damnation,
Deliver us, good Lord.
—*G. K. Chesterton*

The ultimate act of humility is asking God for help.

February 29

Blessed is he whose help is the God of Jacob, whose hope is in the Lord his God, the Maker of heaven and earth, the sea, and everything in them—the Lord, who remains faithful forever.
Psalm 146:5–6, NIV

God,

This is a special date—one that only comes around every four years. So I wanted to take this special time, God, to praise you on your creation. You are so totally incredible! Whenever I watch one of those nature shows on TV, I'm amazed by you all over again. You are the ultimate artist! The colors of all those fish. The way the eagles soar through the sky. And those bugs! Who knew how much complexity and fierceness you built into all those little, tiny bugs?

You must have had a great time creating it all. Thanks for allowing me to enjoy your beautiful work.

If God created everything in nature so quickly, imagine what he's got in store for eternity. Talk about paradise!

My Thoughts & Prayers

What's been on your mind (and heart) this month? Have you had any big answers to prayer? What's your most important prayer request? Use this space to keep track of all that's been going on.

_____

_____

_____

_____

_____

_____

_____

_____

_____

_____

_____

_____

_____

_____

**Stop your anger! Turn from your rage! Do not
envy others—it only leads to harm.**
Psalm 37:8, NLT

God,
    I hate to even admit that I do this, but I
think I sometimes get angry with someone just
because I'm jealous. I haven't really thought about it
much before, but it makes sense. Usually one bad feeling
leads to another. Maybe one of the first steps to stopping
my angry feelings is to stop envying other people. Maybe if
I weren't so preoccupied with wishing I had other people's
looks, talent, friends, money, or whatever, I wouldn't have
so many angry feelings. God, I'm tired of feeling angry with
other people. Help me be content, not angry. Amen.

Negative feelings never travel alone.
They always arrive in groups.

March 2

Love is patient.
1 Corinthians 13:4, NIV

Father,
    I'm really starting to like someone. You know who it is. I can't stop thinking about it—ever. From the time I wake up until I go to bed at night, it's all I can think about. I'm so distracted.
    God, this is my first *big* crush. It feels like I'm going to burst if it doesn't work out, and I'm starting to think the feelings are only on my side. I don't know what to do. It hurts when I think that we might not ever be more than friends.
    Please help me, Father, to know what to do with these feelings. If this isn't going to happen, help me to let go of how I feel and move on. But if there is a chance for us, Father, help me to know how to act and think until we can be more than friends.

*'Tis sweet to court, but, oh how bitter
to court a girl and then not git her.*
—1850s album verse

See to it that no one takes you captive through hollow and
deceptive philosophy, which depends on human tradition and
the basic principles of this world rather than on Christ.

Colossians 2:8, NIV

Dear God,

    People look so hard for the answers to making relation-
ships work. The TV is full of psychologists and psychics and
even preachers promising that their methods or philosophies
can fix any relationship. And some of what they have to say
sounds kind of interesting.

    But I'm starting to understand that your teachings are all
about relationships. The Bible talks about relationships
between husbands and wives, parents and children, and
church members. Your word has helped me know what to do
with anger and fear and attraction. I want to remember that
when I get confused by relationships or when I have questions about what I should do in them, I can turn to you for
help. I want to know your answers before anyone else's.

*God's Word contains the only genuine
blueprint for successful relationships
with Him and others.*

**—Gary Smalley with John Trent,
Love Is a Decision**

Don't praise yourself; let others do it!
Proverbs 27:2, NLT

God,

I've got a friend who brags about himself all the time. It drives me *nuts*. He brags about his stuff, his family, his grades. It's actually kind of sad. It's like he thinks he has to keep reminding us how great he is or we won't like him. Please help him to learn how much you love him so he'll know how much he's worth and he won't feel like he has to keep bragging.

Please also help me to overcome the temptation to pump myself up in front of people. You know that I some-times feel insecure, too. But I don't want to give in to boasting to try to make myself feel better. Let my life speak for itself. Better yet, let my life speak for you. Help me to represent you well and to bring you glory.

Thanks for the person you've made me, Father. Let that person please you.

And so, dear brothers and sisters, I plead with you to give your bodies to God. Let them be a living and holy sacrifice—the kind he will accept. When you think of what he has done for you, is this too much to ask?

Romans 12:1, TNLB

Dear Lord,

It feels like I have nothing to offer you. I'm just one person who lives a very plain, unspectacular life. But that's not true, is it? When I really think about it, I have *everything* to offer you.

When I go to work, I want to have a positive attitude that pleases you.

When I'm at home, I want to treat my parents with respect and try to do my share of the work.

When I'm doing schoolwork, I want to do the best I can because that's what you do for me.

When I'm competing, I want to be a humble winner and a gracious loser; I always want to know that I tried my hardest.

When I'm sitting around doing nothing, I want to spend some time focusing on you.

God, I guess my ordinary, unspectacular life can be a gift to you after all. Please accept it with my love.

Amen.

God delights in transforming the meaningless into the meaningful. Let him into your life, and he will add meaning.

March 6

Quietly trust yourself to Christ your Lord, and if anybody
asks why you believe as you do, be ready to tell him, and
do it in a gentle and respectful way.
1 Peter 3:15–16, TLB

God,
I'm not ashamed of believing in you, but it's hard for
me to talk about it with other people. It's a very personal
thing. Many people don't agree with what I believe, and I
can't always explain things clearly. Most of all, I don't want
to be known as one of those pushy religious types.
When someone asks me about you, though, I want to
be ready to answer. I need to be ready for that because I'm
sure it will happen sometime. When it does, God, help me
to be kind and courteous and to follow your example.
Amen.

*People will ask you about God if they
see him reflected in you and your
actions. Let your life be an
advertisement for God and his word!*

The jailer called for lights, and rushing in, he fell down
trembling before Paul and Silas. Then he brought them
outside and said, "Sirs, what must I do to be saved?"
They answered, "Believe on the Lord Jesus, and you will
be saved, you and your household."
Acts 16:29–31, NRSV

Jesus,

I always thought that to be "saved" I had to follow a
bunch of rules. I thought being saved was about never
missing church, always praying before I went to bed, saying grace at every meal, never swearing, never lying, never
cheating—you know, just being a good person.

But it's much simpler than that, isn't it? It's just about
believing in you. Not just believing that you exist, but
believing you are who you say you are—believing it enough
to put my entire trust in you. That seems so much easier
than what I was doing before. It wore me out trying to
always be on my best behavior so I could be good enough
to be saved.

But in some ways, it seems much harder than what I
was doing before. At least then I felt like I was in control.
I was trying to be good. *I* was trying to be nice. *I* was trying
to rack up enough points to be saved. Now I see that it's all
about you—not me. It's about letting you do the saving,
while I do the trusting.

March 8

For it is by grace you have been saved,
   through faith—and this not from
yourselves, it is the gift of God—not by
   works, so that no one can boast.
   Ephesians 2:8–9, NIV

I am happy because you have accepted me, dear Lord.
Sometimes I do not know what to do with all my
   happiness.
I swim in your grace like a whale in the ocean.
The saying goes: "An ocean never dries up,"
but we know that your grace also never fails.
Dear Lord, your grace is our happiness. Hallelujah!
   —*West African prayer*

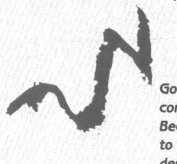

*God's grace can sometimes be a hard
concept to grasp. This is grace:
Because we said yes to his invitation
to life, God gave us what we didn't
deserve and didn't give us what we did
deserve.*

O Lord, you have searched me and known me. You know when I sit down and when I rise up; you discern my thoughts from far away....How weighty to me are your thoughts, O God!
Psalm 139:1–2, 17, NRSV

Dear Lord,

At times, I feel like I just don't connect with anybody. My family is going in all different directions. I like my friends, but I'm not sure they even know who I really am. Some of them seem to want me to be someone I'm not.

I feel so alone, God! I want to feel like I belong to a group of people. I want to feel understood and appreciated by my friends and family. I want to feel like it would make a difference to someone if I just didn't show up one day.

I need to always remember that I'm not alone. You know me and love me and always care about what I'm up to. Help me to always remember that, and please help me to be the kind of friend and family member I want others to be for me.

March 10

Jesus said, "You're blessed when you're at the end of your rope. With less of you there is more of God and his rule."
Matthew 5:3, TM

Dear God,

I don't like being at the end of my rope. I don't like feeling out of control. And with everything that's going on in my life—school, friendships, family, job, sports—it's so easy to feel that way.

Help me to remember that when I feel like I'm cracking under the pressure, when I'm sinking under my burdens, when I'm drowning in stress, you're the one who can rescue me and put me back on my feet.

And I want to ask you something else, too—I know I sometimes forget to spend time with you during my good periods. Help me to run to you all the time—even when things are going smoothly and I'm feeling good. Help me to remember that you're always there for me, not just when things are tough.

God's loving presence isn't just reserved for bad days; it's there for all days.

March 11

> **Give ear, O God, and hear; open your eyes and see the desolation of the city that bears your Name. We do not make requests of you because we are righteous, but because of your great mercy.**
> *Daniel 9:18, NIV*

God,

If the only time I could pray to you and ask for your guidance was after a perfect, sinless day, I'd be in big trouble. It would never happen.

When I pray, God, it's not because I think I deserve anything. I will never be that good. Thank goodness it doesn't work that way. Thank you for listening to me even when I feel like I've completely messed up my life. Thank you that I don't have to earn the right to pray to you. Thank you that you love me enough to listen to me, even when it must sound like I'm just whining, complaining, pouting, and mouthing off.

God, I love you.

Amen.

Everyone has a right to pray. That's a precious gift that God has given all of us. Use it.

Children, obey your parents in the Lord, for this is right.
"Honor your father and mother"—this is the first
commandment with a promise: "so that it may be well
with you and you may live long on the earth."
Ephesians 6:1–3, NRSV

Father,

Sometimes my parents drive me nuts! I want to honor
my parents because you've said to do it, but honestly,
sometimes that's about the only reason I even do it. It
seems to me that people should earn respect and honor.
And you know that there are days when they don't do that.
I wish you would have made the command read: "Honor
your father and mother when they deserve it."

But you didn't. Help me to honor and obey them for
you, God. Help me to love them because you do and
you've asked me to do the same. Help me to accept that I
won't always understand why they do certain things. And,
Father, please help them to be good parents, because that
would help me to be a better kid.

*I think that one reason we're called upon to honor our parents
is because the task that they have of nurturing us, of providing
for us, and of giving us guidance is a huge task. And they are
merely human. They're going to mess up a lot.*
—Rich Mullins

Lord,

You know I don't like some of the things about me and my life. I'm not crazy about some parts of my personality, and I'd really like to change a couple of things about the way I look. And I *really* wish I didn't have to deal with some of the bad stuff that happens to me—like when my family or friends disappoint me.

But I think I figured out that you're using those hard things to shape me into the person you want me to be. I finally get it! Those bad things force me to lean on you more than I would if everything in my life was perfect. I need those things—even though I don't like them.

Thanks, Lord, for helping to mold me, even if you have to use some not-so-nice things to do it.

Do not free a camel of the burden of his hump. You may be freeing him from being a camel.
—G. K. Chesterton

**The heavens are yours, and yours also the earth;
you founded the world and all that is in it.**
Psalm 89:11, NIV

For cities and towns, factories and farms, flowers and trees,
    sea and sky—
Lord, we praise You for the world and its beauty.
For family and friends, neighbors and cousins—
Lord, we thank You for friendship and love.
For kind hearts, smiling faces, and helping hands—
Lord, we praise You for those who care for others.
For commandments that teach us how to live—
*Lord, we thank You for those who help us to understand
    your laws.*
And for making us one family on earth, the children of
    One God—
Lord, we praise You, who made all people different, yet alike.
    —*a Jewish liturgy*

*God gives us so much. It can be easy to take it all for granted.
When you're feeling down and like maybe you don't have much
that's good in your life, take a hard look at the big and little
things that God has blessed you with.*

**But God demonstrates his own love for us in this:
While we were still sinners, Christ died for
us. . . . For if, when we were God's enemies, we
were reconciled to him through the death of his
Son, how much more, having been reconciled,
shall we be saved through his life!**

Romans 5:8, 10, NIV

Dear Lord,

What a thing you did! None of your creation was asking to be with you forever. We weren't smart enough to know we needed you. We thought we could do it on our own. But you loved us too much to let us go, Father. You loved us too much to say, "Fine. Be that way. It's your loss."

It *would* have been our loss—forever. So you sent your Son. He obeyed you and chose to die the death we deserved—all this before we even wanted to be with you. What a thing you did! Thank you, my God, for loving me that much, even before I loved you. Help me to remember and to love you now.

March 16

But encourage one another daily, as long as it is called Today, so that none of you may be hardened by sin's deceitfulness.
Hebrews 3:13, NIV

Father,

So many people in my life are hurting. I see them at school, at work, at church—even at home. Life can be hard for so many different reasons. Father, I want to help people to feel better, not worse. I want to be a positive influence, to build up people around me. I want to be an <u>en</u>courager, not a <u>dis</u>courager.

I want to be a good listener who helps others, God. Someone who people know they can turn to for motivation. Help me to be a positive person, one who focuses on others and not just on myself. I want to be a good listener. And, Father, please give me wisdom to know the right words to say to encourage the people you bring into my life. Amen.

When someone does something good, applaud! You will make two people happy.

—Sam Goldwyn

**For the Lord is good and his love endures forever;
his faithfulness continues through all generations.**
Psalm 100:5, NIV

I arise today
Through the strength of heaven:
Light of sun,
Radiance of moon,
Splendor of fire,
Speed of lightning,
Swiftness of wind,
Depth of sea,
Stability of earth,
Firmness of rock.

I arise today
Through God's strength to pilot me:
God's wisdom to uphold me,
God's eye to look before me,
God's ear to hear me,
God's word to speak for me,
God's hand to guard me,
God's way to lie before me. . . .

—*attributed to St. Patrick of Ireland*

March 18

Paul asked, "Did you receive the Holy Spirit when you believed? Did you take God into your mind only, or did you also embrace him with your heart? Did he get inside you?"

Acts 19:2, TM

God,

You're a very important part of my life. I believe in you—I really do. But I'm not always sure how deep our friendship is. And that's not because of you. It's because of me.

Have I taken you into my mind only? Do I believe in you just because it seems like the right thing to do? Because my parents do? Because I've been taught to? Or have I taken you into my heart, into my soul, into the part of me that is real and lasting?

I want more than just a casual friendship with you. I want to have a relationship that is open and honest, totally trusting, and completely personal. It won't be easy for me. I've never had a relationship that deep before. Please be with me in more than just my thoughts. Be with me in my heart. Fill me up with you. Amen.

No matter what your parents believe, there comes a time when you must decide for yourself whether you want to live for God. It must be your choice.

Then I heard the voice of the Lord saying, "Whom shall I send, and who will go for us?" And I said, "Here am I; send me!"
Isaiah 6:8, NRSV

Father,

I have something I have to admit. There's a part of me that's afraid to say, "Here am I; send me." I think it's because I'm afraid of how you might answer. What if you send me to some filthy, poor, dangerous place where I don't want to go? What if you tell me to do some kind of work that I don't like or that's too hard for me? What if you take away all my hopes and plans for the future and make me do something gross and unglamorous?

See what I mean? I know my fears are silly—but they're real to me.

Help me believe that you want only what's best for me. Help me to trust that whatever you have in store for me is the thing that will fulfill me and give my life meaning and purpose. Help me remember that you don't want to ruin my life or make me miserable. You want to love me and take care of me. So . . . "Here am I; send me." And please, God, give me the strength to really mean it when I say it.

God will never send you where you shouldn't go. He will never ask you to do what you cannot do. He loves you, remember?

March 20

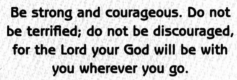

**Be strong and courageous. Do not
be terrified; do not be discouraged,
for the Lord your God will be with
you wherever you go.**
Joshua 1:9, NIV

God,

I know Joshua 1:9 tells us to be strong, but I'm not always strong. I don't get terrified very often (mostly just when I think about the future), but I do get discouraged. A lot. It's seems like something's always happening to discourage me—things don't go the way I'd hoped or I don't measure up to other's expectations (or, even worse, my own expectations for myself) or life moves in a direction other than the one I'd planned on.

With all of that going on, it's easy to get discouraged. It happens way too often if I'm not careful.

Help me to remember, Lord, that no matter what is happening in my life and no matter which direction things are going, you are there with me. I may not always feel you and I may not see you, but you are there. As long as I don't forget that, I *can* be strong. With you, I can keep moving forward.

Woe to the man who fights with his Creator. Does the pot argue with its maker? Does the clay dispute with him who forms it, saying, "Stop, you're doing it wrong!" or the pot exclaim, "How clumsy can you be!"?
Isaiah 45:9, TLB

Father,

The Bible asks what right I have to complain about the way you made me. Are you kidding? I have every right! After all, I am *me*, and I don't understand why you made me the way I am. Am I just one of your jokes? Did you enjoy making me so much less than perfect just so you could have a good laugh?

I'm sorry for going off like this, but, God, I just do *not* understand why you didn't make me differently. There are so many ways you could have improved me. Is that too much to ask?

Please forgive my attitude. I know I sound crazy and unthankful. It's just that right now, I don't really like the way I am. And it's easiest to blame it on you, the one who made me. But I will try to stop second-guessing your design and will try, instead, to let you shape me the way you want. Thank you for making me and loving me.

Though it is often hard to believe, when God looks at you he sees the most beloved, most precious, most wonderful of his creations—his very own child.

After all, salvation is not given to those who know what to do, unless they do it. The day will surely come when at God's command Jesus Christ will judge the secret lives of everyone, their inmost thoughts and motives; this is all part of God's great plan, which I proclaim.

Romans 2:15–16, TLB

God,

Whenever I'm tempted to do something that I know I shouldn't or whenever I actually do it, my conscience kicks into gear. I can practically hear in my heart a voice telling me what's wrong. At the same time, whenever I try to do something kind, I hear that same voice encouraging me to do more things like that.

Until now, I never thought that my conscience—that voice inside my head and heart—might have something to do with you. But it seems obvious. You made me that way, with a strong sense of your values and guidelines. Thank you for that—it's a gift that I want to pay more attention to in the future. Please help me to do that. Amen.

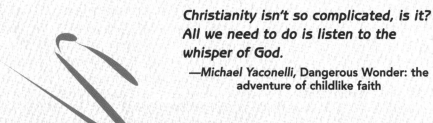

Christianity isn't so complicated, is it? All we need to do is listen to the whisper of God.

—Michael Yaconelli, Dangerous Wonder: the adventure of childlike faith

Depend on it: God keeps his word even when the whole world is lying through its teeth.

Romans 3:4, TM

God,

Is it true that you will never go back on your word, never break your promises, never lie to me about anything?

It's almost impossible to believe. It seems like everyone breaks their word at some point—friends, teachers, coaches... even my parents. I know they don't usually mean to disappoint me, but it's still pretty hard to take.

But you—I know I can always trust you, God. Thank you for the fact that you will never disappoint me. It's such a relief to have someone I know I can always rely on no matter what.

God is the only friend you will ever have who is incapable of disappointing you.

March 24

**God is kind, but he's not soft. In kindness
he takes us firmly by the hand and leads
us into a radical life change.**
Romans 2:4, TM

Lord,

When I was little, I used to want my parents to hold my hand when we were going someplace. It made me feel safe. I was glad to have someone take me by the hand and give me some direction.

I feel the same way about you, God. I know some people don't want to let you have a say in how they live, but it makes me feel safe. I know some people think they're too mature to be led around like a baby. They think they know which direction to head in. They think they've got it all figured out.

Well, I don't. I'm still figuring out so many things. So I'm glad that you're here, holding my hand, leading me along the way, taking me on a radical journey that will be like nothing I've ever experienced.

Three times I pleaded with the Lord to take it away from me. But he said to me, "My grace is sufficient for you, for my power is made perfect in weakness." Therefore I will boast all the more gladly about my weaknesses, so that Christ's power may rest on me.

2 Corinthians 12:8–9, NIV

Dear Lord,

I ask you for a lot of things. Lately, I think I've been asking you for more than ever. Maybe it's because I'm learning to trust you more than ever. I hope so. Something I've noticed, though, is that you don't always give me what I ask for. Sometimes, nothing happens. At other times, it's like you're just saying "no."

The strange thing is, as I look back on some of the things I've asked for, I'm really glad you didn't give them to me. I wouldn't want them now. I can see that they would have been all wrong for me.

So now I realize you didn't ignore me; you were looking out for me. I now know you're working for my best interests—even when you don't give me what I want. Thanks that even when you refuse me, you're loving me.

I have had prayers answered—most strangely so sometimes—but I think our heavenly Father's loving-kindness has been even more evident in what He has refused me.

—Lewis Carroll

March 26

A hot-tempered person starts fights
and gets into all kinds of sin.
Proverbs 29:22, NLT

Father,
    I don't know what to do with all this anger I've been feeling. I want to set it down, but I'm not sure I can. Someone has hurt me very deeply—someone I trusted, someone I liked. It's been a while now, and I want to move past it, but it's hard. Please help me to let it go.
    I know, Father, that you are in control of everything. You love me. You protect me. You provide for me. Help me to trust you with my anger. Help me to leave what happens to this person in your hands. I trust you to do what's right. Thank you for the peace I know you can give.

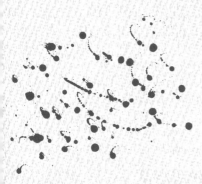

Anger is never without a reason,
but seldom with a good one.
—Benjamin Franklin

**People can tame all kinds of animals and birds and
reptiles and fish, but no one can tame the tongue.
It is an uncontrollable evil, full of deadly poison.**
James 3:7, NLT

God,

I can really hurt people with my words. I've seen the looks on their faces when I say something stupid or just plain mean. The weird thing is that I don't always do it on purpose. Sometimes I start out with the best intentions. I'm really trying to help—but then my words get all tangled up and just come out wrong.

Why does that happen, God? Why can't I control my words? I can understand when I'm trying to cause someone pain. That's easy. But why do I hurt people without even trying?

Help me, God, to control the words that come out of my mouth. Help them to honor you and be helpful to others. Help me to be kind with my words—to build people up instead of tearing them down.

March 28

And whatever you do, whether in word or deed,
do it all in the name of the Lord Jesus, giving
thanks to God the Father through him.
Colossians 3:17, NIV

Lord Jesus Christ,
alive and at large in the world,
help me to follow and find you there today,
in the places where I work,
meet people,
spend money,
and make plans.
Take me as a disciple of your kingdom,
to see through your eyes,
and hear the questions you are asking,
to welcome all others with your trust and truth,
and to change the things that contradict God's love,
by the power of the cross
and the freedom of your Spirit.
—*John V. Taylor*, A Matter of Life and Death

It's hard for me to answer "What would Jesus do?"
if I'm not trying to see life and people as Jesus
saw them. I must work to find Jesus' way.

**Praise God, who did not ignore my
prayer and did not withdraw his
unfailing love from me.**
Psalm 66:20, NLT

Father,

I listen to some people pray, and they're asking you for such big and important things—peace in the world, an end to hunger, the spreading of the gospel. And then I listen to myself pray, and I feel like I'm asking for such selfish, unimportant things: "Help me to do well on the test." "Help people to like me." "Help me to be able to come up with enough money to buy a car."

But, God, I know you hear and answer my prayers. I know you care about me—even my "little" desires. You love me enough to listen to the things I really care about—even if they're not huge or important to the world. Thank you, Father, for listening to me and paying attention to my prayers.

March 30

> Trust in the Lord with all your heart;
> do not depend on your own
> understanding. Seek his will in all
> you do, and he will direct your paths.
> *Proverbs 3:5–6, TM*

God,

I want to understand life. I want to be able to figure out why people do the things they do, even the things that seem so stupid, so cruel, or so strange. I want to know how the stars stay suspended in the sky for ages and ages, doing their mighty dance with one another. I want to understand how the earth was placed a perfect distance from the sun so that we neither freeze nor burn to death.

But I will never know those things. So help me to learn the things that are within my grasp . . . like how to love others, how to live joyfully, how to be a good friend, how to be faithful and loyal, and how to have integrity. Let me gracefully accept my limits of understanding. At the same time, let me try to understand all that I am capable of. Amen.

The wisest people are not the ones who know everything. They are the ones who admit that they know very little while they still try to learn as much as they can.

Before the Passover celebration, Jesus knew that his hour had come to leave this world and return to his Father. He now showed the disciples the full extent of his love.... So he got up from the table, took off his robe, wrapped a towel around his waist, and poured water into a basin. Then he began to wash the disciples' feet and to wipe them with the towel he had around him.... "No," Peter protested, "you will never wash my feet!" Jesus replied, "But if I don't wash you, you won't belong to me."
John 13:1, 4–5, 8, NLT

Jesus,

I'm trying to imagine the scene when You washed the disciples' feet. I've always found it a little embarrassing to think about You wrapped in a towel, bent over a bunch of dirty, smelly feet, washing each one gently in a pan of water. It just doesn't seem appropriate to picture the Lord of heaven doing something so everyday, so intimate, so grubby.

My Lord, after an ordinary day, my heart is soiled with the grime of selfishness. I hate to let anyone get close to me for fear they'll catch a whiff of the stale, foul smell of self.

Jesus, pour Your clean water into the pan. Get out Your towel. Wash me clean.

—*Ellyn Sanna,* By the Water: A Collection of Prayers for Everyday

My Thoughts & Prayers

What's been on your mind (and heart) this month? Have you had any big answers to prayer? What's your most important prayer request? Use this space to keep track of all that's been going on.

_____

_____

_____

_____

_____

_____

_____

_____

_____

_____

_____

_____

_____

_____

_____

_____

**The way of a fool seems right to him, but
a wise man listens to advice.**
Proverbs 12:15, NIV

Father,

It's April Fool's Day, which—of course—is a fun day, but it's got me thinking about something serious—what exactly it means to be foolish. The Bible has a lot written about fools, especially in Proverbs. Solomon must have known a whole bunch of fools, and he describes them really well. But, Father, can I tell you something kind of scary? I sometimes recognize myself in those descriptions. I can be so foolish sometimes.

I don't want to be a fool. The Bible says fools are people who aren't teachable—people who think they already know it all. Please don't let me be so proud that I don't think I can learn something new. Help me to always be ready to listen and gain new understanding.

Wise men don't need advice. Fools won't take it.
—Benjamin Franklin

I, wisdom, live with prudence, and I attain knowledge
and discretion. The fear of the Lord is hatred of evil.
Pride and arrogance and the way of evil and perverted
speech I hate. I have good advice and sound wisdom;
I have insight, I have strength.
Proverbs 8:12–14, NRSV

Lord,
I want to become a wise person, someone who has
good advice for friends and can make difficult decisions.
I don't want to be some know-it-all who drives everyone
crazy. I don't want to always say annoying things like,
"Say, did you know...." or "Well, I've experienced that
before...."

I want a quiet wisdom that others respect. God,
please help me to seek out wisdom. And let me have
the humility not to have to advertise my wisdom to
others. And I promise to use my wisdom to live my life
the way that you think is best. Amen.

*Don't confuse intellect and wisdom. Intellect has no value
unless it is accompanied by wisdom. Wisdom has value
whether or not it is accompanied by intellect.*

> But God demonstrates his own love for us in this: While
> we were still sinners, Christ died for us....For if, when
> we were God's enemies, we were reconciled to him
> through the death of his Son, how much more, having
> been reconciled, shall we be saved through his life!
> *Romans 5:8, 10, NIV*

Dear God,

This is an important time to be a Christian. I want to be able to explain you to my friends. I want to be able to say, "God works in this way," or "God answers me like this," or "I know all about God."

But I can't. There are so many things that I just do not get. That used to bother me. It made me feel stupid when someone challenged or questioned my faith. But now it makes me feel safe. By realizing and recognizing that you are beyond understanding, I'm able to see that you really are God. If I could put you in a box or define you or pin you down, you wouldn't be God.

It's true—I cannot understand everything you do. But I can love you, and I can follow you, and I can try to help others love and follow you, too. Please show me how.

April 4

My Lord Jesus Christ,
Two graces I beg you to grant me
before I die:
The first is that in my lifetime
I may feel, in my soul and in my body,
as far as possible,
that sorrow which you, tender Jesus,
underwent in the hour
of your most bitter passion;
the second is that I may feel in my heart,
as far as possible,
that abundance of love with which you,
son of God,
were inflamed, so as willingly to undergo
such a great passion for us sinners.

—*Carlo Carretto*, I, Francis

Jesus experienced two things for your sake—the agony of death in order to save you and a love so strong that he willingly endured the pain and sorrow of that death. What more could you ask for in a friend?

April 5

So I recommend having fun, because there is nothing better for people to do in this world than to eat, drink, and enjoy life. That way they will experience some happiness along with all the hard work God gives them.

Ecclesiastes 8:15, NLT

Oh God, this is going to be a great day. The sun is shining, the sky is blue, and I don't have to take any tests all week. Help me to have a great week just enjoying life and making the best of my free time. Thanks for this feeling of peace. Amen.

April 6

Jesus said, "Stop judging others, and
you will not be judged. For others will
treat you as you treat them."
Matthew 7:1–2, NLT

Father,

    I so often feel like people think I'm not good at anything. I'm not fast enough. Not smart enough. Not neat enough. Not creative enough. Not athletic enough. Not funny enough. Not attractive enough. Not strong enough. Not popular enough. Not nice enough. Not cool enough. Not everything and anything enough.

    It hurts when people say those things to me or when I think they're thinking them about me. It makes me want to criticize them back, which makes them criticize me right back, which makes me want to criticize them right back. . . . It's a bad cycle! I guess the only way to stop it is to not participate. But, man, that's a tough one. I think I'm going to need a lot of your help on this. Please help me to give others—and myself—a break and not criticize.

Everyone knows that no human is perfect, but somehow it's always easier to see someone else's faults than it is to admit your own.

April 7

Save me, O God, for the waters have come up to my neck. I sink in deep mire, where there is no foothold; I have come into deep waters, and the flood sweeps over me. I am weary with my crying; my throat is parched. My eyes grow dim with waiting for my God.
Psalm 69:1–3, NRSV

God,

Why does my life seem like such a roller coaster—going up and down and looping all around? Frankly, God, I'm a little sick of the ride. I have a few good weeks when things go smoothly and I feel so connected to you, then things fall apart and everything that can go wrong does. During those low times, I cry out to you, and I feel like I can't get through. I feel like my words just hit a wall and drop to the ground.

Are you there? Do you hear me? In my mind, I know you are there listening. But in my heart, where my emotions are going crazy, I'm not sure.

Help me stand on your firm truth, God, not on my fickle feelings. Please get me out of this hole I'm in. Amen.

Even when you're down and feeling all alone, God is there with you. He can handle your feelings of despair and anger and abandonment. But you must open up to him before he can help you.

April 8

After the Sabbath, as the first light of the new week dawned, Mary Magdalene and the other Mary came to keep vigil at the tomb. Suddenly the earth reeled and rocked under their feet as God's angel came down from heaven, came right up to where they were standing. He rolled back the stone and then sat on it. Shafts of lightning blazed from him. His garments shimmered snow-white. The angel spoke to the women: "There is nothing to fear here. I know you're looking for Jesus, the One they nailed to the cross. He is not here. He was raised, just as he said."

Matthew 28:1–3, 5, TM

Jesus,

Where are you now? The whole resurrection story seems so unbelievable to me (a lot of things about you seem unbelievable), but if I believe in you—and I do—then I have to believe this part of your life, too. It stretches my faith, but if I can't accept the resurrection, then I can't accept anything about you. So, Jesus, I know you're somewhere, alive and well, but where? I can't even begin to imagine what it will be like when I meet you. What will you look like? I've always wondered. None of the paintings I've seen seem very real. What will you sound like? I wonder if your voice is loud or soft, strong or gentle.

No matter—you are alive. That is what gives my faith meaning. And I'm living for the day when I will finally see you in person. Thank you for loving us enough to sacrifice yourself for us. Amen.

**We can't round up enough containers to hold everything God
generously pours into our lives through the Holy Spirit!**
Romans 5:5, TM

Father,
　　I can't believe all the things you give me
every day. I don't just mean my family, home,
food, and friends. Those are great, but what you
give is so much more than that.
　　When I feel lonely, you comfort me with your
presence.
　　When I feel rejected by a friend, you remind
me that you accept and love me.
　　When I feel stressed out, you help me to
take a deep breath and regain my composure.
　　When I feel sad, you let me know that joy is
somewhere around the corner.
　　Those are the types of things that no one
else can offer me and that I can't buy anywhere.
Thank you for thinking of all those things that you
give me each day.

*The only way to experience an overflowing cup is to let God be
part of your life. He will fill you over and over and over again.*

April 10

God knew what he was doing from the very beginning. He decided from the outset to shape the lives of those who love him along the same lines as the life of his Son.... After God made that decision of what his children should be like, he followed it up by calling people by name.

Romans 8:29, TM

God,

I once heard a saying that the most beautiful word in the human language is a person's own name. I think that's totally true.

At school, when I have a new teacher who remembers my name, it means something to me. When I meet new kids in class and they remember my name, it matters. At home, when my mom or dad asks me to do something and says my name first, I usually listen more closely. My name makes me feel important—like I'm somebody. When people call me by name, it feels like they're talking to *me*, not to just any old person.

Thank you for calling me by name and for treating me as a somebody. Thank you for always knowing who I am. I love it. Amen.

April 11

> Now if you obey me fully and keep my
> covenant, then out of all nations you will be
> my treasured possession.
>
> *Exodus 19:5, NIV*

Lord, you are like a wild flower. You spring up in places where we least expect you. The bright colour of your grace dazzles us. When we reach down to pluck you, hoping to possess you for our own, you blow away in the wind. And if we tried to destroy you, by stamping on you and kicking you, you would come back to life. Lord, may we come to expect you anywhere and everywhere. May we rejoice in your beauty. Far from trying to possess you, may you possess us. And may you forgive us for all the times when we have sinned against you.

—*Henry Suso*, The Exemplar

It is a terrible tragedy to be possessed by another person. It is a wonderful gift to be possessed by God.

> *Jesus replied, "You must love the Lord your God with all your heart, all your soul, and all your mind."*
> *Matthew 22:37, NLT*

Father,

I'm wondering how long I'm going to have to wait for the love of my life. I feel like I'm ready. I think about it all the time. I really want to share my time with someone special. I want to give myself to someone who will love me deeply. But I don't see that happening any time soon.

Even when it does happen, I want that relationship to make my connection with you stronger. Until then, help me to focus on you and be patient. Maybe you're saying I need more time now to get to know you better and to get to know myself better. If so, help me to do what I must to be ready for that special relationship when the time comes. Help me to fall in love with you even more. And help me to be patient as I wait for that special someone to come into my life.

Because God is always with his children, time spent alone is really time alone with him. Don't waste it.

But he was wounded and bruised for *our* sins. He was beaten
that we might have peace; he was lashed—and we were
healed! *We*—every one of us—have strayed away like sheep!
We, who left God's paths to follow our own. Yet God laid on
him the guilt and sins of every one of us!
Isaiah 53:5–6, TLB

God,

I've always heard that Jesus "died for my sins." In fact,
I've heard it so many times that it doesn't really mean anything to me anymore. It seemed to lose its importance. It
was like, big deal, Jesus died for me.

But I never understood that he not only died for my
sins but actually took my sin onto him. Every time I've lied,
every time I've hurt someone, every time I've been rude,
every time I've cheated—Jesus took that into himself so
that when God looked at him, he saw all my wrongdoing.
Jesus didn't just die *for* me . . . he died *because* of me. And
he did it willingly. That's almost too much to grasp. I never
realized. Thank you.

*Jesus was not a victim at the
cross. He was a volunteer. He went
and willingly died for you. He didn't
have to. He wanted to.*

April 14

When he had received the drink, Jesus said, "It is finished."
With that, he bowed his head and gave up his spirit.
John 19:30, NIV

God,
    Sometimes I think about that moment on the cross when Jesus said, "It is finished!" I think about the invitations that were sent out at that moment to join you in heaven forever if we would just admit our need and trust in Jesus. I never could have reached you on my own. You knew that, so you sent Jesus to make it possible.
    I've never regretted saying yes to your invitation, God. Since that day, I've realized even more how much I need you—what a waste my life would have been without you! I'm still blown away that you would do that for me. Thank you, God.

"Paid in full" was written and circled in blood across the debt of my sin. The payment required was death, but God paid it instead. And he paid it for no other reason than the fact that he wanted to.

—John Fischer, On a Hill <u>Too</u> Far Away: Putting the Cross
Back in the Center of Our Lives

The grass withers and the flowers fall,
but the word of our God stands forever.
Isaiah 40:8, NIV

Dear Lord,

Things change so quickly in the world. Fashions are different from year to year and season to season. Music, movies, and TV shows are constantly changing. I have different teachers and classes from year to year. My friends change. My work sometimes changes. It just seems like there's never anything constant about my life!

But it's good to know that you never change, that you always have the same love, the same compassion, the same concern for people. And it's also good to know that your word never changes, that I can go to the Bible now, next year, or in 50 years, and it's still going to tell me that love is the best thing, that God created me, that Jesus saved me, that truth is a solid rock to base my life on. I need the stability that you offer, God, because everything else is constantly shifting. Amen.

It's important to have an anchor that holds you steady in life's shifting waters. Let God be that anchor.

April 16

**Don't sin by letting anger gain control over you.
Think about it overnight and remain silent.**
Psalm 4:4, NLT

God,

One of the hardest things for me to do is control my anger. It seems to just flare up inside of me and explode... especially with my family. Sometimes it's justified. But sometimes it's not.

No matter what the case, I want to learn how to control my anger instead of letting it control me. Your word gives some pretty good advice on how to do that—*wait* before acting or speaking. If I could just give myself a few minutes, or even a few seconds, before reacting, I'd probably be more rational and calm, and I'd probably hurt fewer people with my angry words. Please teach me the art of waiting before exploding. Amen.

*It's not a sin to be angry, but it is a sin
to let anger control your life.*

April 17

Now, no one is likely to die for a good person, though someone might be willing to die for a person who is especially good. But God showed his great love for us by sending Christ to die for us while we were still sinners.

Romans 5:7–8, NLT

God,

When I read those words, I want to cry. I don't feel like I'm a really awful person, but I also know I'm not perfect. I've messed up plenty of times in my life. And certainly there is nothing I can offer you that you don't already have—except myself.

So why would you go to the cross for me—and why would you do it before I'd cleaned up my act and decided to follow you? That was a huge risk on your part. What if I'd decided not to follow you? Would you have still felt like I was worth dying for?

I don't understand, God. That kind of love is too much for me to comprehend. But I am so grateful that you love me like that. There is no way I can ever say "thank you" or "I love you" enough.

Even if you were the only person on earth, Jesus would have still gone to the cross. That's how much he loves you.

April 18

> Come, everyone, and clap your hands for
> joy! Shout to God with joyful praise! For
> the Lord Most High is awesome. He is the
> great King of all the earth.
>
> *Psalm 47:1–2, NLT*

God,

I can get so excited about you—especially when I'm praising you with a group of other Christians. Sometimes I just love to worship you out loud. You are God. You created all, and you love *me*. I have so much to celebrate when I think of you.

I praise you, God, for all you have given to me, all you have done for me. You are everything that matters in the universe. Your power and your love together make you the God of all people. Help me to sing your praises in the way that you enjoy most. Help me to please you with my worship of you.

A big part of loving God is proudly celebrating that love out loud.

April 19

Therefore, since we have been made right in
God's sight by faith, we have peace with God because
of what Jesus Christ our Lord has done for us. Because of
our faith, Christ has brought us into this place of highest
privilege where we now stand, and we confidently and
joyfully look forward to sharing God's glory.
Romans 5:1–2, NLT

Dear God,

There is nothing better than meeting people you want to be friends with and then discovering that they feel the same way about you. But it doesn't always work that way. Lots of times, the feelings are just one-sided and someone gets hurt.

God, I'm so glad that my friendship with you isn't that way. When I decided I wanted to get to know you and follow you, it would have been devastating if you'd said, "Sorry. Not interested. You just don't fit the description of what I'm looking for in a friend."

But when I looked for you, you were right there, waiting for me with open arms. Right away, I'd never felt so loved in my life. It doesn't get any better than that!

April 20

Dear Lord,

Lord, I'm so mixed-up! I honestly don't understand why such terrible things happen on this planet. People shooting at other people in schools and on the streets. Planes full of men, women, and children going down. All that war and hunger I see on TV. I know you're powerful enough to stop it. What's the deal?

But if I'm really honest, Father, I guess I also know that you give us freedom and that some people use that freedom to make wrong choices. I know sometimes I also make wrong choices that can hurt people.

I know that you are good, God. I know that you are powerful. Help me to trust that you know what you're doing with this freedom thing, even when I see violent stuff that scares and confuses me.

And please help me to make choices that won't hurt people. Amen.

April 21

There is something else meaningless that occurs on earth: righteous men who get what the wicked deserve, and wicked men who get what the righteous deserve.

Ecclesiastes 8:14, NIV

God,

I don't get it. Why do good things happen to bad people and bad things happen to good people? It doesn't seem fair. It doesn't seem loving. It doesn't seem like you're paying attention to the world or like you care. At least, not all the time.

Shouldn't the good people, the people who follow you and your teachings, have good things happen to them? And shouldn't bad people, the people who hurt others, have bad things happen to them? That seems like an obvious no-brainer.

But you are not an obvious God. There are a lot of things I don't understand—and this is one of them. I know that someday I'll understand. For right now, give me the faith to remember and believe that you are in control, no matter how it may seem. You never promised that only good things would happen to good people . . . you only promised to love them and to always be with them.

Through both good times and bad, it is important to remember that God is always present and always loving. During the good times, he rejoices with us. During the bad times, he weeps with us. Never, never does he leave us to rejoice or weep alone.

Let the whole earth sing to the Lord! Each day proclaim
the good news that he saves. Publish his glorious deeds
among the nations. Tell everyone about the amazing
things he does. Great is the Lord! He is most worthy of
praise! He is to be revered above all gods.

1 Chronicles 16:23–25, NLT

If my lips could sing as many songs
as there are waves in the sea:
if my tongue could sings as many hymns
as there are ocean billows:
if my mouth filled the whole firmament with praise:
if my face
shone like the sun and moon together:
if my hands
were to hover in the sky like powerful eagles
and my feet
ran across mountains as swiftly as the deer;
all that would not be enough
to pay you fitting tribute,
O Lord my God.

—a Jewish prayer

Now we see but a poor reflection as in a mirror;
then we shall see face to face. Now I know in part;
then I shall know fully, even as I am fully known.

1 Corinthians 13:12, NIV

God,

I've got to admit that sometimes I just don't get you. I'll think I have you figured out—what you're going to do, who you are, what you're up to—then something happens that completely changes my ideas about you. You're way beyond my ability to understand you. I guess that sort of comes with being God of the universe!

Thank you that you're bigger than I am. Thank you that I can't pin you down or figure you out. If I could, then you wouldn't be much of a God. Help me, though, to trust you when you do what I don't expect. Help me to remember that you love me and that you're always working for my best. Thank you that one day I will know you completely and we'll be together.

Like the wind, God cannot be predicted as he moves upon his creation and in our lives. He shakes our religious ideas and breaks apart our brittle concepts, our neat categories and answers.

—Harold Myra, *Living by God's Surprises*

April 24

Do you think anyone is going to be able to drive a wedge between us and Christ's love for us? There is no way! Not trouble, not hard times, not hatred, not hunger, not homelessness, not bullying threats, not backstabbing, not even the worst sins listed in Scripture.

Romans 8:35, TM

Dear Lord,

Relationships can be so confusing. I was *positive* that I'd be friends with certain people forever and now we're not at all close anymore. Romances start out great and seem like real, forever kinds of things and then they're over. I guess there's no way to know what's going to happen with anyone else in my life.

Some of my relationships have ended because of a disagreement or crisis. Sometimes they've ended for no real reason at all—it just seemed to happen. The worst part is when someone gets hurt because of the ending. All those feelings of betrayal and unkindness are pretty hard to handle.

So I love that our relationship is a forever kind of thing. Thank you for being loyal and faithful and for loving me so much that I don't have to worry about losing you. It's bad enough when one of my human friendships breaks apart; I don't think I could handle it if my relationship with you went wrong. I'm glad I don't have to worry about that.

A faithful friend is an image of God.
—French proverb

April 25

> **God saw all that he had made, and it was very good. And there was evening, and there was morning—the sixth day.**
> *Genesis 1:31, NIV*

God,

You created a beautiful world. It's true that people don't always take good care of it, and that some places are no longer the way you intended them to be. Help me to remember that the creation, the world—the trees and rivers and oceans and fields—are yours. You made them. You designed them. You brought them into being. If I can remember that, God, then maybe I will be more careful about how I treat the earth and the things that live in it. I don't worship creation, God; only you should be worshiped. But I do appreciate it. And I'll try to treat it with the care and respect it deserves. Amen.

The creation is God's gift to humankind. Such a precious gift is surely worthy of our protection and care.

April 26

Dear Father,

I know that you want to be involved in my life—to help me make decisions, to help me mature into a loving person, to help me stay away from things that aren't good for me. Usually, I can live with that.

But sometimes, I forget that you only want what's best for me, and I start to hold on to my life pretty tightly. It's hard to let you guide and teach me. Most of the time I'm convinced that I know what's best for me.

When I do that, though, things start falling apart. The more I try to steer the car of my life, the more crazy the ride gets. Still, it feels reckless to give you the wheel and say, "OK, here you go. Where to next?" But that's what I want to do because I *know* you love me and want what's best for me. I'm sorry about always trying to take the lead; it's a pretty hard habit to break.

The best person to have guiding a journey is the one who drew the map.

> Jesus said, "Do for others what you would like
> them to do for you. This is a summary of all
> that is taught in the law and the prophets."
> **Matthew 7:12, NLT**

God, I've always been taught that I should do unto others as I would have them do unto me. I always thought that meant that I shouldn't do certain things *to* people. Like I shouldn't be mean, shouldn't talk about people behind their backs, shouldn't criticize them. That kind of stuff.

But now I realize that it means a lot more than that. It also means I should do certain things *for* people. I should show them kindness, should reach out a helping hand, should include them, should encourage them.

Help me to remember that being your child isn't so much about what I *can't* do but about what I *can* do. That tiny shift in focus makes me realize that following you isn't drudgery; it's joy!

*Being God's child isn't about following
a list of rules; it's about loving others.*

April 28

> But the Lord said to Samuel, "Do not consider his appearance or his height, for I have rejected him. The Lord does not look at the things man looks at. Man looks at the outward appearance, but the Lord looks at the heart."
>
> *1 Samuel 16:7, NIV*

Lord,

No matter what anyone says, appearance matters in this world. The most beautiful people are chosen as models. The best-looking kids are the first to be asked to dances. The tallest and strongest are chosen as leaders.

God, the way I look matters to others. And to me. I'm sorry to say that I often wish I looked differently.

And God, I can't deny that the way others look matters to me, too. Like I can't imagine dating someone who isn't attractive. I know that's shallow, and I know that's not the way you want it. So I'm going to try to change the way I think. Help me to remember that outward appearance isn't important, no matter what the world or others say. It's the inside—the heart, the soul, the character of a person—that matters in others (and in myself). Help me to develop my inner appearance and to see the inner beauty in others.

We all want people to look beyond our outer appearance and to recognize our inner worth. If we want others to do that for us, then we must also be willing to do that for them.

Woe to those who call evil good and good evil, who put
darkness for light and light for darkness, who put bitter for
sweet and sweet for bitter.

Isaiah 5:20, NIV

Dear God,

It can be hard to tell what's true sometimes. So many
lies about life are disguised to sound good and right—it
can get pretty confusing. Especially now, when gods and
angels and spirituality and meditation are so popular, and
so many people are talking so much about it. Who's right
and who's wrong? Everything sounds so good, but I know it
can't all be true.

God, I don't want to judge anyone or condemn anyone
for what they believe. I just want you to give me the wisdom to tell the difference between truth and lies, between
good and evil, between dark and light, between bitter and
sweet. Then please give me the courage to follow the right
path once you've pointed it out to me. Thank you.

*There are many paths in life that look
right, sound right, feel right, and
seem right. But never assume. Always
take the time to ask God for guidance. It will save you from many
wrong turns, many heartaches, and
many mistakes.*

God said, "My gracious favor is all you need. My power works best in your weakness." So now I am glad to boast about my weaknesses, so that the power of Christ may work through me.

2 Corinthians 12:9, NLT

Behold, Lord, an empty vessel that needs to be filled. My Lord, fill it. I am weak in the faith; strengthen me. I am cold in love; warm me and make me fervent that my love may go out to my neighbor. I do not have a strong and firm faith; at times I doubt and am unable to trust you altogether. O Lord, help me. Strengthen my faith and trust in you. In you I have sealed the treasures of all I have. I am poor; you are rich and came to be merciful to the poor. I am a sinner; you are upright. With me there is an abundance of sin, in you is the fullness of righteousness. Therefore I will remain with you of whom I can receive but to whom I may not give. Amen.

—*Martin Luther*

If we were strong enough to serve God on our own—to do everything he wanted—we wouldn't need God. In fact, we would be God. It's our weaknesses that make us human and show his power through us.

My Thoughts & Prayers

What's been on your mind (and heart) this month? Have you had any big answers to prayer? What's your most important prayer request? Use this space to keep track of all that's been going on.

_____

_____

_____

_____

_____

_____

_____

_____

_____

_____

_____

_____

_____

_____

_____

_____

_____

_____

May 1

The heavens declare the glory of God;
the skies proclaim the work of his hands.
Day after day they pour forth speech;
night after night they display knowledge.

Psalm 19:1–2, NIV

God,
when I look at the sky,
I can tell what You have been doing.
The sun, the moon, and the stars
      show that You keep things
      going all the time.
Every morning the sun shows us
      that You are still on the job.
Each night is Your promise
      for another day.
I don't need to hear Your voice.
I can hear what You are saying
      when I see what You do.

—*Eldon Weisheit*, Psalms for Teens

*Just as a painting proves the existence
and ability of a painter, creation proves
the existence and ability of God.*

May 2

**Stop trusting in man, who has but a breath
in his nostrils. Of what account is he?**
Isaiah 2:22, NIV

Dear Father,

There are certain people I trust. I believe that they care for me and that they want what's best for me. I don't look at them as gods—just as people I can lean on and count on and go to for advice and companionship.

I think that you want me to have this kind of relationship with them. That's what friendship and family are all about, right?

But in terms of trusting people as a whole to give me what I need (forgiveness, love, a sense of completeness, that sort of thing) and to tell me the truth (especially that a relationship with you is the most important thing in life), I know it won't ever happen. I need to turn to you for those things. It's not that people are so bad—it's just that they aren't you. They simply can't give me all that I need. I'm glad I have you, and I'm glad I have people in my life who love me, care about me, and help me learn about you. Amen.

May 3

Be gentle and ready to forgive; never hold grudges. Remember, the Lord forgave you, so you must forgive others. Most of all, let love guide your life, for then the whole church will stay together in perfect harmony.

Colossians 3:13–14, TLB

Jesus,

Teach me how to forgive other people as much as you've forgiven me. It seems impossible sometimes. One of the hardest things for me to do is to forgive a friend who has betrayed me. That's the worst kind of pain there is—having someone you love and trust turn their back on you. I'm always glad when the problem gets worked out and the friendship is OK again, but I'm not always as glad about having to forgive the other person. I want them to remember what they did to me, and I want them to feel bad about it for a while. Is that really so wrong? I know, I know—it's immature, but I'm being honest.

Forgiving is so hard. Forgetting is even harder. I don't know if I can ever forgive other people like you've forgiven me, but I'm willing to try if you will show me how. Amen.

Forgiveness is an action of love, total love.
—Madeleine L'Engle

For God wants you to be holy and pure and to keep clear of all sexual sin so that each of you will marry in holiness and honor.
1 Thessalonians 4:3–4, TLB

God,

Lately, abstinence is a hot topic of conversation in the news. There are all kinds of campaigns with people making pledges to keep themselves virgins until they're married. They seem very serious about it.

It's pretty clear what you want—you want sex to be saved for marriage, where it can be shared by two people who are committed to each other for life.

That's not exactly what the media shows, though. Even with all the abstinence campaigns going on, the media—movies, TV, and even music—is filled with images of unmarried people jumping into bed with each other. It's pretty impossible not to notice.

If and when I get married, I want to be able to give myself to my spouse as a gift, which means I need to be careful and wise with that gift, starting right now. God, I don't want to think of sex cheaply, like most of the world does. I want to think of it as a wonderful gift from you that I should treat with honor and respect.

You're the gift. Your spouse is the recipient. Take care of the present.
—Kevin Johnson, What Do Ya Know?

May 5

Don't love the world's ways. Don't love the world's goods. Love of the world squeezes out love for the Father. Practically everything that goes on in the world—wanting your own way, wanting everything for yourself, wanting to appear important— has nothing to do with the Father. It just isolates you from him. The world and all its wanting, wanting, wanting is on the way out—but whoever does what God wants is set for eternity.
1 John 2:14–15, TM

Dear Lord,

You've warned me about the world over and over. I don't always see the danger. I guess since this is the only life I've known, I don't always recognize what is harmful. Besides, the most harmful things are usually subtle. They slip into my mind without my even realizing it.

The worst one is the idea that I'm the most important person there is and so I'm entitled to have whatever I want. TV shows and movies try to get me to believe that all the time. I can see the dangers of drinking, drugs, casual sex . . . but the danger of believing in a me-first world isn't really as obvious.

God, I'll keep trying to figure out how to live in the world without letting its messages fill my head. Maybe the best thing I can do is fill my head with your message so there's no room for anything else.

The best way to keep enemies out is to make sure there is no empty space where they can get in.

May 6

**If you claim to be religious but don't control
your tongue, you are just fooling yourself, and
your religion is worthless. Pure and lasting
religion in the sight of God our Father means that
we must care for orphans and widows in their
troubles, and refuse to let the world corrupt us.**
James 1:26–27, TLB

God,

I don't know any orphans or widows that I can take care of—but I'm guessing that you would be just as happy if I offered a helping hand or tried to love anyone who is in some kind of need. There are some places I could help out—the local food pantry, a homeless shelter, the nursing home—and I'm sure that they are always in need of extra hands.

From what I can tell, God, you ask only two things of me—that I reach out to other people and that I remain faithful to you. It's easy: love others and love you. It always comes back to those two things. Thanks for keeping Christianity clear and simple. Amen.

Just because you cannot do everything, you should not neglect doing what you can. Remember, little is much when God is in it.

—Dr. Harold J. Sala, **Heroes: People Who Made a Difference in Our World**

Great and holy God
awe and reverence
fear and trembling
do not come easily to us
for we are not
Old Testament Jews
or Moses
or mystics
or sensitive enough.
Forgive us
for slouching into Your presence
with little expectation
and less awe
than we would eagerly give a visiting dignitary.
We need
neither Jehovah nor a buddy—
neither "the Great and Powerful Oz" nor "the man upstairs."
Help us
to want what we need
You
God
and may the altar of our hearts
tremble with delight
at
Your visitation

amen.

—*Frederick Ohler, "Awe-full"*

Then Saul said to Samuel, "I have sinned. I violated the Lord's command and your instructions. I was afraid of the people and so I gave in to them."

1 Samuel 15:24, NIV

Dear Lord,

One of the things I really want for myself is to be strong enough to stand up for what I believe in—even when others don't agree with me. Usually I can do that. But sometimes I just can't. Or I don't—I'm not always sure which. I find myself going along with the crowd and going against you because it's easier, because it's convenient, or because I'm afraid of what others will think or say about me if I don't. I know that's not exactly a good, brave way to feel—but it's the honest, raw truth.

God, help me to be brave. Give me the courage to follow you, even when you are leading me in a different direction than others are going. And forgive me for all the times I haven't done that in the past. Amen.

Following God isn't as easy as following the crowd, but good things often don't come easily.

Physical exercise has some value, but spiritual exercise is much more important for it promises a reward in both this life and the next.

1 Timothy 4:8, NLT

God,

I know that it's important for me to stay physically healthy. It's not always easy to find the time to work out, but I try. And I know I should eat better than I do—it's just so easy to grab fast food when I'm in a rush. Physical health is important to me, God, so I try to take care of myself.

So why don't I do the same with my spiritual health? It's much easier to ignore the spiritual part of me than the physical. If I get physically flabby, it shows. If I get spiritually flabby, who will ever know? You will—and other people eventually will, too, when my outward life starts reflecting my inward life.

Show me some ways that I can stay spiritually healthy. Praying each day really helps me, but I'd like to do more.

Keeping your spirit healthy requires just as much commitment, energy, and dedication as keeping your body healthy, but the rewards last much, much longer.

May 10

But when the kindness and love of
God our Savior appeared, he saved us,
not because of righteous things we had
done, but because of his mercy.
Titus 3:4–5, NIV

Thank you, Father, for always being merciful. You always give to your people, and you always bless our families. Thank you for blessing me and mine with your mercy, Lord. You have shown great mercy to me O Lord, according to your lovingkindness. Thank you for the multitude of your tender mercies in my life.

I rejoice over the fact that your mercy is from everlasting to everlasting upon all those who fear you in a reverential way. Lord, it was when I began to fear and reverence you that I experienced your mercy and you granted spiritual wisdom to me. Now I know that your lovingkindness and your mercy are better than life to me. . . .

—Praying God's Promises

May 11

Samuel said, "Now then, stand still and see this great
thing the Lord is about to do before your eyes!"
1 Samuel 12:16, NIV

Father,
    I hardly have time to stand still. There is always so much jammed into my schedule, and it usually feels like I'm two steps behind. When I do stand still, God, what should I expect to see from you? I've never exactly noticed heavenly fireworks or heard a thundering voice. What kind of great things should I be looking for?
    Maybe I'm just expecting big things that I'll see right away but it's really the small things that I should be looking for—a new friendship, a long conversation, something amazing in nature. I guess first I need to find the time to stand still and then I need to have an open mind, because I'm sure there are great things going on all the time, and I'm just too busy to notice them. Give me standing-still time, Lord, and then give me receptive ears and eyes. I don't want to go through life without seeing all the great things you are doing.

It's an old saying, but a true one: Good things do come in small packages. God gives us lots of great little things. Only those who are willing to look in the unexpected places will be able to recognize and enjoy them.

**A capable wife who can find? She is far
more precious than jewels. . . . Her children
rise up and call her happy.**
Proverbs 31:10, 28, NRSV

Lord, Mother's Day always makes me think about my mom.
Thank you so much for her. I don't always treat her the way
I should. I don't always thank her enough. I don't always
help her enough. But even though I don't always show it, I
do love and appreciate her. I can't imagine what it must like
to be a mother and be responsible for another human
being for so many years. Just the thought of it scares me,
and yet Mom does it.

God, I love her. And I want to be able to tell her and
show her how I feel. Please help me to never take her
presence for granted. Amen.

*Do not forget that God chose to enter this
world through someone with the least
appreciated, least promoted, most overworked
position on earth . . . a mother. Surely mothers
are blessed among all people because of this.*

May 13

Jesus said, "You're blessed when you get your inside world—your mind and heart—put right. Then you can see God in the outside world."
Matthew 5:8, TM

Jesus,

Even though no one else can see inside my thoughts (thank goodness!), I know you can. It's not always pleasant to look at, is it? It can be a little embarrassing having you know all that I'm thinking. It's pretty hard to keep my mind and heart focused on you. It's a lot easier to just go with the flow and think about the things the world says are important—success, money, power, sex, and possessions.

But when I think about those things in the wrong way—when I think that they are the key to happiness—then the whole world starts to look pretty bad. I start becoming cynical about life. I feel like everything and everyone is out of control.

When I start to feel that way, that's when I know that I've lost touch with you on the inside, that I've let my thoughts stray too much from you and your teachings. God, help me to know you in my heart and in my mind and in my soul. I know only when you're there inside with me will I be able to see the world through your eyes.

May 14

Jesus said, "You are the salt of the earth. But what good is salt if it has lost its flavor? Can you make it useful again? It will be thrown out and trampled underfoot as worthless. You are the light of the world—like a city on a mountain, glowing in the night for all to see. Don't hide your light under a basket! Instead, put it on a stand and let it shine for all."

Matthew 5:13–15, NLT

God, when I taste the "food" around me that is on tel-evision, on the radio, and in the movies, I feel like choking. So much of it isn't true. And lots of it mocks you and those who believe in you.

God, when I peer out at the pictures around me that are in magazines, in advertisements, and on videos, some-times I feel like I'm walking in total darkness. So much of it lacks any sort of light at all. And so much of it denies your existence as anything other than a fantasy.

I want to bring good and positive things to people, God. I want to be the salt and light to the world. We all need to see some positive things. I don't want to come on so strong that anyone chokes on your goodness or feels blinded by your love. I just want to bring out all the flavors and colors of your world.

A world without flavor and color is a world without hope.

May 15

Why am I discouraged? Why so sad?
I will put my hope in God! I will praise
him again—my Savior and my God!
Psalm 42:5–6, NLT

Father,

I'm so depressed today. These downs just creep up on me now and then, and they affect everything I do and say. Nothing seems to help, especially having people say, "Just get over it."

So I'll do the only thing that makes sense: I'll start thinking about you and everything I know about you. Your love, your kindness, your patience, your acceptance—there's no way I can think about those things and stay depressed. It's not possible.

Be patient with me, God. I'm trying to get through this. And I'll be patient, too, and know that you will help me if only I call to you. Amen.

You may not have the power to erase your blues, but you do have the power to redirect your focus.

> David said to the Philistine [Goliath], "You
> come against me with sword and spear and
> javelin, but I come against you in the name
> of the Lord Almighty, the God of the armies
> of Israel, whom you have defied."
>
> *1 Samuel 17:45, NIV*

Jesus,

I've known the tale of David and Goliath since I was little. Great story. But I'm only just beginning to see how I fit into it. I feel like David a lot of times, like I'm fighting against this huge giant without even a chance of winning. I fight against peer pressure, against my jealousy, against my desire to be popular, against the world's view of success, and I think to myself, "Who am I kidding? I can never win this war!"

I forget that I'm not fighting alone. You are with me. And the goal of this war isn't to knock anyone down or wipe out a population—it's simply to stand firm with the truth. God, I think I can do that with your help. Thanks for being there to fight alongside me.

Why would people try to fight life's battles on their own when they have the world's strongest weapons—the truth and love of God—on their side?

May 17

Why are you downcast, O my soul? Why so disturbed within me? Put your hope in God, for I will yet praise him, my Savior and my God.
Psalm 42:5–6, NIV

Lord, there are people who have curled up and died in a corner for no reason other than they lost hope. When there is no hope, there is no life. Without hope we give up—we lose our will to fight, to trust, to live.

There are too many people in this world today who have begun to lose hope—those who hunger for life's basic needs but see no relief; those who see too many problems and cannot find a solution.

When I begin to lose hope, too often I have forgotten that hope is inseparably connected to love and faith . . . your love which powerfully confirms that you are not only the bringer of life, but you *are* Life . . . faith that receives love humbly and enables me to respond with hope to even the most complicated problems. . . .

Lord, we do not hope in ourselves, our technology, our governments, our laws, our tenacity, our courage, or our will. . . . We hope in you. *Amen.*

—*Thomas G. Pettepiece*, Visions of a World Hungry

Anything worth putting your hope in must be trustworthy, true, reliable, consistent, and fair. Put your hope in God.

May 18

O Lord, our Lord, the majesty of your name fills the earth! Your glory is higher than the heavens. When I look at the night sky and see the work of your fingers—the moon and the stars you have set in place—what are mortals that you should think of us, mere humans that you should care for us?

Psalm 8:1, 3–4, NLT

God,

   When I look at the amazing mountains, the immense ocean, the stars at night. When I realize how *HUGE* the universe is, I wonder—do you really notice me? Do you really care? The universe is so indescribable, beyond belief, incomprehensible.

   And yet, you love me. *You love me.* In the whole world, there's nothing as awesome as that. How can I help but love you in return?

The universe may be amazing beyond belief, but you are truly loved by God and that is the most amazing creation of all.

May 19

**Don't be quick-tempered, for
anger is the friend of fools.**
Ecclesiastes 7:9, NLT

God,

There are some people in my life who are angry all the
time. Or, at least it seems that way. When I'm with them,
I'm always afraid that I'll do or say something that will make
them mad. I feel like I'm walking on eggshells when I'm
around them.

I wonder if I ever make people feel that way—if they're
afraid to be around me because they never know how I'll
react. God, I hate it when people are quick-tempered with
me—like if my parents yell before knowing what really happened. I certainly don't want to be that way to other people! Give me the maturity I need to stay in control of
myself. Thank you.

*People are drawn to joy, not anger.
Choose wisely which you will be.*

My dear brothers and sisters, be quick to listen, slow to speak, and slow to get angry. Your anger can never make things right in God's sight.
James 1:19, NLT

God,

I can never be reminded enough that I should sometimes just keep my mouth shut and simply *listen*. That would prevent probably half of the problems I get myself into. And it would make me a better friend. People want friends who will listen to them, not just talk about themselves. If I could only remember to listen first, then speak later, I would probably be a lot happier and content. But I usually forget, so please help me. Somehow, help me to keep my mouth still and my ears alert. Amen.

Listening is one of the greatest skills a person can have.

May 21

Oh, the joys of those who do not follow the advice of the wicked, or stand around with sinners, or join in with scoffers. But they delight in doing everything the Lord wants; day and night they think about his law.

Psalm 1:1–2, NLT

O Lord . . . save us
from hotheads
that would lead us
to act foolishly,
and from cold feet
that would keep us
from acting at all.
—Peter Marshall

It's tough to decide which is worse—acting too quickly or not acting at all. But even if moving in one direction seems wrong and moving in another direction seems worse, simply standing still could be the worst of all. When you have to make the choice about your direction, just remember it's always right to walk straight ahead on the path of truth. Walk toward God.

Thus says the Lord, your Redeemer, the Holy One of Israel: I am the Lord your God, who teaches you for your own good, who leads you in the way you should go. O that you had paid attention to my commandments! Then your prosperity would have been like a river, and your success like the waves of the sea.

Isaiah 48:17–18, NIV

My Lord,

Well, I've done it again. I've decided that my way is best, and I've gotten myself into a bad situation that isn't going to be easy to get out of.

Even though I know your commands and guidelines are for my own good, sometimes they just don't fit in well with what's going on around me. It's easier to ignore your advice and do my own thing. And in the end, of course, I always regret it. It's so much easier to make decisions *after* I can see the consequences.

God, I want peace back in my life. And that will only happen when I start following you again. Help me, please. Amen.

No matter how many times we lose our footing, take our own path, or momentarily lose sight of God's direction, he is always there ready to set us upright, help us find the true path, and give us a glimpse of his glorious love.

May 23

Let the Word of Christ—the Message—have the run of the house. Give it plenty of room in your lives.
Colossians 3:16, TM

God,

My life is very full. I have so many activities and hobbies and responsibilities that it's amazing they all fit into my day. Actually, it often doesn't fit into my day. Nothing really gets too much attention because I'm dividing myself among so many different things. I'm sorry that you and your words don't get more attention than anything else in my life. It ends up being just another thing I have on my to-do list.

I know it shouldn't be that way. If anything should have my full attention, it's you. I'd love to give you the run of the house in my life. I'm just not exactly sure how. But thank you for sticking with me while I learn.

God doesn't want to stay in the entryway of your life. He wants to come in and inhabit every room fully.

Christ is the exact likeness of the unseen God.
Colossians 1:15, TLB

Dear Father,
  Even though I've known them a long while, at times I look at my friends and think, "Do I really know you at *all*?" After all, how do you *really* know a person? The more time I spend with them, the more I watch how they act and listen to how they speak, the more I get to know their families and other friends, then the more I feel that I know them.
  God, sometimes I think about you and wonder, "Do I really know you?" After all, if Jesus was the exact likeness of you, then of course it makes sense to learn more about Jesus if I want to learn more about you. To get to know the Father, I will get to know the Son.

Cling tightly to your faith in Christ, and always
keep your conscience clear. For some people
have deliberately violated their consciences;
as a result, their faith has been shipwrecked.

1 Timothy 1:19, NLT

Steer the ship of my life, good Lord, to your quiet har-
bour, where I can be safe from the storms of sin and con-
flict. Show me the course I should take. Renew in me the
gift of discernment, so that I can always see the right
direction in which I should go. And give me the strength
and the courage to choose the right course, even when the
sea is rough and the waves are high, knowing that through
enduring hardship and danger in your name we shall find
comfort and peace.

—*Basil of Caesarea*

*On the open seas of this life, God's
word is the only chart available to
keep us from drifting aimlessly and
crashing into the shore.*

May 26

For surely I know the plans I have for you, says the Lord,
plans for your welfare and not for harm, to give you a
future with hope. Then when you call upon me and come
and pray to me, I will hear you. When you search for me,
you will find me; if you seek me with all your heart, I will
let you find me, says the Lord.

Jeremiah 29:11–14, NRSV

God, it's good to know that you have plans for my life
because I am totally confused about the future. I'm not
planning on sitting back lazily, just waiting for you to deliver me wherever I'm supposed to be. I don't think you're
that kind of God. I think you want me to be in control of
my life, to make decisions, to be active. But for right now,
while I'm in the dark about what's up ahead, it's nice to
know that you're in control. I'll do my best to make plans
and seek out what seems to be the best for me, and I'll
try to figure out what you have planned, too, so that I'll be
on the right track.

Thanks for being involved in my life and for caring
about my future. Amen.

*God knows where you are going, and he knows where you will
end up. But you still have a choice about whether that is what
you will do.*

May 27

Jesus said, "Do you want to stand out? Then step down. Be a servant. If you puff yourself up, you'll get the wind knocked out of you. But if you're content to simply be yourself, your life will count for plenty."

Matthew 23:11–12, TM

God,

For as long as I can remember, I've wanted my life to matter. I want to do something significant, something important, something that makes a difference. And I thought in order to do that, I'd have to do something big— something that other people would notice.

But you tell me that's not true. You say I can make a difference and that my life will count for plenty if I'm just myself. That's so cool. It takes off a lot of the pressure to be someone I'm not. Maybe the problem with doing "big" things is that it's so easy for pride to creep in. If I accomplished something amazing, I know I'd feel proud. And everyone knows that pride comes before a fall. Thanks for letting me know that I can be myself and still do great things, even if they seem small and sort of insignificant. That makes me feel more excited about my life. Amen.

It's not the size of your accomplishments that matter; it's the attitude behind them.

 # May 28

God is our refuge and strength,
an ever-present help in trouble.
Therefore we will not fear, though the earth give way
and the mountains fall into the heart of the sea,
though its waters roar and foam
and the mountains quake with their surging.

Psalm 46:1–3, NIV

Lord,

That's what life feels like sometimes—like an earthquake, an explosion, a tidal wave, a crumbling mountain. It feels wild and out of control.

But you are always there, watching out for me, holding on to me, sheltering me, loving me.

So I'll try not to be afraid. I'll try to think about you and your strength. I'll try to remember that you are God and you are in control. When my life starts to quake and my world seems to explode, please help me to remember that you're with me.

While the world seems to be caving in around you, God will meet you where you least expect it—in the eye of the storm, right there in the middle of your own tornado.

May 29

**Do not be grieved, for the joy
of the Lord is your strength.**
Nehemiah 8:10, NLT

Lord, I thank you for your joy which is my strength. When I come to the end of my journey, I look forward to your words, "Well done, thou good and faithful servant: thou hast been faithful over a few things, I will make thee ruler over many things: enter thou into the joy of thy Lord."

Thank you for taking the spirit of fear away from me and replacing it with a spirit of power, love, and a sound mind that greatly produces joy in my innermost being. I thank you that your kingdom does not consist of meat and drink, but of righteousness, peace, and joy in your Holy Spirit. . . .

—Praying God's Promises

*Joy isn't a feeling that comes and goes.
We choose to live in joy by trusting in
God. And that joy makes us strong.*

Jesus said, "If you love me, obey my commandments."
John 14:15, NLT

God,

I really do love you, but I'm beginning to realize that that's easier to *say* than to actually *do*. Being a hypocrite isn't hard—all you have to do is say one thing and do another.

It feels like there are tons of hypocrites all around me. Teachers who say they'll never play favorites, and then do anyway. Friends who say they'll never betray me, but do anyway. Bosses who promise they'll treat everyone fairly, but don't. And even me, who believes in you but doesn't always act like it.

God, help me be honest, trustworthy, and reliable so that I always reflect my love for you in my actions. Help me to be someone other people can count on. Help me to be a person whose words and actions are alike. I don't want to just *say* I love you. I want to really do it. I want to be as loyal to you as you are to me. Amen.

True love isn't expressed in hollow words. It's shown through firm commitment.

May 31

Lord,

Thank you for making me just the way I am. I'm not the best-looking, but that doesn't matter. At least not to my friends and my folks or to you. I'm not the smartest kid in the class, but I do my homework, study hard, and do extra assignments when I think it will help. I am all that you made me to be, so I have a lot to work with.

And maybe someday I'll be the best at something. I've got a bunch of time to get good at all sorts of things. So please help me to remember that high school is not always going to be my world. One day I'll be in college or have a job or have a family, and every so often I'll get to do something really great.

Right now, all I need is patience! Thank you.

My Thoughts & Prayers

What's been on your mind (and heart) this month? Have you had any big answers to prayer? What's your most important prayer request? Use this space to keep track of all that's been going on.

_____

_____

_____

_____

_____

_____

_____

_____

_____

_____

_____

_____

_____

_____

_____

_____

_____

_____

_____

_____

> But when he, the Spirit of truth,
> comes, he will guide you into all truth.
> *John 16:13, NIV*

Father,

I want to know the truth about everything I can. The more I pay attention to what's being said in the world around me, the more I realize how much of it is lies or just plain wrong. I'm afraid that I'm believing some wrong things now—just because I've heard them so often. I don't want to be deceived, Father. I really want to know what's true.

Thank you for giving me your truth through Jesus, through the Bible, and through your Spirit. Help me to keep looking for it and finding it and believing it—even when it's hard to understand or it seems too good to be true. And, most important, Father, help me to live what I know to be true. Amen.

How often have I said to you that when you have eliminated the impossible, whatever remains, however improbable, must be truth?
—Sir Arthur Conan Doyle

You are holy, Lord, the only God, and your deeds
    are wonderful.
You are strong, you are great, you are the
    most high, you are almighty.
You, Holy Father, are King of heaven and earth.
You are Three and One, Lord God, all good.
You are good, all good, supreme good, Lord God,
    living and true.
You are love, you are wisdom. You are humility,
    you are endurance.
You are rest, you are peace.
You are joy and gladness, you are justice and moderation.
You are all our riches, and you suffice for us.
You are beauty, you are gentleness.
You are our protector, you are our guardian and defender.
You are courage, you are our haven and hope.
You are our faith, our great consolation.
You are our eternal life, great and wonderful Lord,
God almighty, merciful Savior.

—St. Francis of Assisi

June 3

Jesus said, "Heaven and earth will disappear,
but my words will remain forever."
Mark 13:31, NLT

Dear God,

Sometimes life feels so temporary—especially when I think about history. So many people have lived and died on this earth. I'm sure when they were alive, it seemed like they would live forever. I know it feels that way for me. But they didn't. They lived their years and died.

Thank you for bringing me into a relationship with you that will last forever. Thank you for giving me things—like your word and relationships with your people—that will last forever. Thank you for preparing a forever home for me with you. Thank you that my existence isn't really temporary, even if my time on this planet is.

*The Bible holds the only
information that will still
matter to us a million years
from now.*

**For everything there is a season, and a
time for every matter under heaven.**
Ecclesiastes 3:1, NRSV

Lord,

I am so ready for this summer. I thought the
school year would *never* end. It was long and hard
and full of things I could never have predicted. I
can't believe everything you brought to me
throughout this year. Thank you so much.

Lord, I want this to be my best summer ever.
I want to relax and sleep late and have the time of
my life. Thank you for summer. Thank you for
warm weather. Thank you for freedom from
school.

Help me, though, Lord, not to take a vacation
from you this summer. Help me to take you with
me everywhere I go and to honor you with everything I do. I want to have a great summer—but
with you along, too!

*Every new season brings a new opportunity to
see how God will show us his love in new ways.*

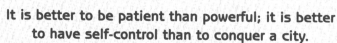

June 5

It is better to be patient than powerful; it is better to have self-control than to conquer a city.
Proverbs 16:32, NLT

Father,

Why is so much of life about waiting for the next thing? I don't like to wait. I don't like to put off good things when I could have them right now. Waiting seems like such a waste of time. If a thing is worth having, why isn't it worth having right now?

But, God, you've got me waiting for so many things I want. And since that's your will for me for now, help me to be patient. Help me to believe with all of my heart that you know best and that your timing makes the most sense. Help me never to run ahead of your plans for my life.

A wise man does not try to hurry history. Many wars have been avoided by patience and many have been precipitated by reckless haste.
—Adlai Stevenson

 **June 6**

Jesus said, "This is a large work I've called you into, but don't be overwhelmed by it. It's best to start small. Give a cool cup of water to someone who is thirsty, for instance. The smallest act of giving or receiving makes you a true apprentice."
Matthew 10:42, TM

God,

I wish I could change the world. When I hear about children who starve to death, when I hear about people being killed in wars, when I hear about young mothers dying from AIDS . . . well, I wish I could do something to make it better, to make life good for everyone.

That's impossible, of course. I know that. But if I can't change the world, is there any way I can at least make a difference? Matthew 10:42 says that just giving a cup of cool water to someone who is thirsty matters to you, God. That seems like it can't be right. It's such a small thing. But if you said it, it must be true. I guess even big things start small, and even helping someone in a small way can make a big difference. So please help me to see the thirsty people in my life. Help me to know what they're thirsty for so I can help them. Amen.

Wishing you could change the whole world is noble, but actually changing your own tiny corner of the world is nobler still.

June 7

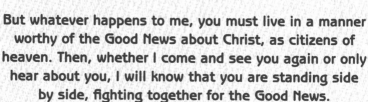

But whatever happens to me, you must live in a manner worthy of the Good News about Christ, as citizens of heaven. Then, whether I come and see you again or only hear about you, I will know that you are standing side by side, fighting together for the Good News.

Colossians 1:27, NLT

Christ, be with me, Christ before me, Christ behind me,
Christ in me, Christ beneath me, Christ above me,
Christ on my right, Christ on my left,
Christ where I lie, Christ where I sit, Christ where I arise,
Christ in the heart of every one who thinks of me,
Christ in every eye that sees me,
Christ in every ear that hears me.
    Salvation is of the Lord,
    Salvation is of the Christ,
    May your salvation, O Lord, be ever with us.
        —St. Patrick of Ireland

The Christian knows that Jesus Christ is the answer to every question, the reassurance to every fear, the only hope for every human heart.

June 8

So don't get tired of doing what is good. Don't get discouraged and give up, for we will reap a harvest of blessing at the appropriate time.
Galatians 6:9, NLT

Dear Lord,

I have a confession that you already know. Sometimes, I get tired of the whole religion thing. I even get tired of reading my Bible and talking to you. It can become such a rut—so boring. And when I get bored with it, I have a harder time not giving into temptation and doing things you don't like.

God, please wake me up. Get me excited again about my relationship with you and your words in the Bible. Remind me of everything you've done for me. Give me the energy and focus to keep serving you by helping others and showing them your love. Father, I don't want to be bored (or boring!). Let me see why all of this matters so much.

Getting bored with our Christianity doesn't mean Christianity doesn't work. It means we need to find a new way to approach our relationship with God.

Jesus answered, "I am the way and the truth and the life. No one comes to the Father except through me."

John 14:6, NIV

O Lord Jesus Christ, you are the Way, the Truth and the Life. We pray you allow us never to stray from you, who are the Way, nor distrust you, who are the Truth, nor to rest in any one other thing than you, who are the Life. Teach us, by your Holy Spirit, what to believe, what to do, and how to take our rest.

—*Desiderius Erasmus*

His name is the only name that will take you from earth to heaven when you die. And it won't be your achievements or your fame or your fortune that will get you there. You will be granted entrance because you accepted the free gift of eternal life—nothing more, nothing less, nothing else.

—*Charles R. Swindoll, The Grace Awakening*

# June 10

But remember this—the wrong desires that come into your life aren't anything new and different. Many others have faced exactly the same problems before you. And no temptation is irresistible. You can trust God to keep the temptation from becoming so strong that you can't stand up against it, for he has promised this and will do what he says.
1 Corinthians 10:13, TLB

God,

I don't know what it was like 20, 200, or 2,000 years ago, but it's hard for me to believe that there were as many things to deal with then as there are now. There are so many messages out there telling me to do whatever I want, grab whatever I need, say whatever I feel.

God, some of the stuff doesn't really tempt me—like drinking and drugs. That's stuff that I know how to say no to. It's the less obvious messages that are hard for me, ones like "You're the most important person in the world" and "You should possess anything you desire."

Sometimes the temptation is almost too much! You promise to help me stand against those things. Well, I'm counting on that promise because I'm already struggling, and I'm sure it will just get worse as I get older and the world moves faster and faster. Stay with me, God.

The modern world offers up lots of temptations, and at times, it may seem impossible to fight them. Just remember that God is always there ready to fight the battle with you.

June 11

Jesus said, "What do you think? If a man owns a
hundred sheep, and one of them wanders away, will
he not leave the ninety-nine on the hills and go to
look for the one that wandered off?"

Matthew 18:12, NIV

Lord, I sometimes wander away from you. But this is
not because I am deliberately turning my back on you. It is
because of the inconstancy of my mind. I weaken in my
intention to give my whole soul to you. I fall back into
thinking of myself as my own master. But when I wander
from you, my life becomes a burden, and within me I find
nothing but darkness and wretchedness, fear and anxiety.
So I come back to you, and confess that I have sinned
against you. And I know you will forgive me.

—*Aelred of Rievaulx*, Prayers of St. Aelred

*When we find ourselves wandering away from
God, whether it's on purpose or not, it's nice
to know that God's seeking us out to bring us
back into the safety he offers.*

June 12

> The Lord is a stronghold for the oppressed, a
> stronghold in times of trouble. And those who know
> your name put their trust in you, for you, O Lord,
> have not forsaken those who seek you.
>
> **Psalm 9:9–10, NRSV**

God,

   I'm learning that following you doesn't make my life perfect. There are still some pretty dark and rough days. It bothers me when people think that life should be smooth and easy just because you're a part of it. Those kind of people just don't get it.

   Thank goodness you are there beside me, holding me up during the bad times. It's wonderful knowing that you are watching over me all the time. Thank you for making the rough times more manageable and less lonely.

People who say that a Christian's life should be perfect are mistaken. God doesn't promise to make life trouble-free. He only promises to walk with you throughout the trouble.

June 13

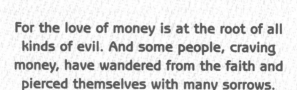

For the love of money is at the root of all
kinds of evil. And some people, craving
money, have wandered from the faith and
pierced themselves with many sorrows.
1 Timothy 6:10, NLT

Father,

My feelings about money scare me. Once in a
while, I'll suddenly realize that I've been thinking about
money—*a lot*. I want the things I can buy with it. I want
the security of having lots of it. I want the control over
my own life that would come from not having to worry
about it.

But, God, I don't have a lot of money. And even if I
did, I wouldn't want it to control me. I've seen too many
people letting their greed for money lead them away
from what's right. God, please help me to think about
money in the right way. Help me to know what to give
to get money—and what not to give up for it. Help me
to always care about pleasing you more than about getting money.

When money speaks, the truth keeps silent.
—Russian proverb

Children, do what your parents tell you.
This is only right.
Ephesians 6:1, TM

God,

I've heard "honor your father and mother" for as long as I can remember. I understand why you said it, but it can be pretty hard. Father's Day is coming up, and I've been thinking about my parents a lot.

I'm ready to be on my own, to make my own decisions and choose my own path. I don't think my parents are ready to let go yet, though. They still want to tell me what to do and how to live. They think I'm too young to make decisions about my life. Every now and then, things totally blow up because of that.

I know my parents only want what's best for me. And even though they sometimes make mistakes, I have to admit that they're usually right in the end. I'll be on my own someday. Until then, give me the grace to respect and honor my parents. They deserve it more than anyone else. Amen.

You don't choose your family. They are
God's gift to you, as you are to them.
—*Desmond Tutu*

June 15

God,

    I want to thank you for my dad. You and I both know he's not perfect. He's only human, after all. And with you as the model of a perfect father, he's got a lot to live up to. But I know he loves me and wants the best for me.

    God, I'm not sure why, but it's so important to me to know that he's proud of me. I want to know he's happy with who I am and the things I can do. Sometimes there's friction between us, and I'm afraid he's disappointed in me. Help me to lead the kind of life he can be proud of. But most of all, help me to make *you* proud of me.

June 16

**You will keep in perfect peace all who trust
in you, whose thoughts are fixed on you!**
Isaiah 26:3, NLT

Father,

I've noticed something pretty simple. I'm happiest when I'm just doing what comes next without worrying about all the things I have to do after that. It can be hard to think that way, but that's when I feel right. I can't do anything about that other stuff anyway. So why not trust you to take care of it all while I do what you've put in front of me right now? Why use up all my energy freaking out about things I can't even control?

Thank you so much, God, for letting me figure that one out! It's going to be so much easier now, knowing I can trust you with anything I can't control. Help me to enjoy each minute as you give it to me and just keep going. And thanks again!

> Do not be afraid when some become rich,
> when the wealth of their houses increases.
> For when they die they will carry nothing
> away; their wealth will not go
> down after them.
> **Psalm 49:16–17, NRSV**

Jesus,

I think it's kind of funny that so many people call you a great person and a great teacher, but then ignore a lot of what you lived and taught—like the fact that money and power and fame don't count for anything in the end.

Almost everything I've worked for in school is so I can get a good job someday and live a comfortable life. And I'll admit it—lots of times I read about these people who have millions of dollars, thousands of fans, and a face that is known all over the world, and I think to myself, "Wouldn't that be nice?"

I hope you'll help me to remember that those things aren't important and, in the end, they count for nothing. If I do end up having money or being well known, I want you to show me how to use it to help others and not just to satisfy myself. Thanks.

Thank you, Lord, for silence.

The silence of great mountains and deserts and prairies.

The silence of the street, late at night, when the last travelers are safely home and the traffic is still. The silence of my room, which enables me to hear small sounds—a moth fluttering against the windowpane, the drip of dew running off the eaves of the roof, a field mouse rustling through dry leaves like an impatient clerk in search of a missing file.

Can there be complete and absolute silence?

Perhaps not. But the silence that permits small sounds to manifest themselves, small creatures to make themselves known, is a silence to be thankful for.

—*Ruskin Bond, "For Silence,"* To Live in Magic

To hear God, you must be silent.
The silence will speak volumes.

Dear Father,

    If your purpose for my life is a sure thing, already decided, then do my actions really make any difference? Do my thoughts and attitudes really matter? Am I significant at all?

    Even though I don't understand it, I know that *I* matter—that what I think matters, that what I do matters. I know that I have choices to make. You don't sit up in heaven and pull on my strings as if I'm a puppet.

    Thank you for giving me the freedom to make my decisions—both good and bad. I know that you notice and care about me, so it must be hard to watch when I make a wrong decision. And thank you for also keeping your hand on the world and all that happens. Amen.

What you do with your life is a choice.
**—Dr. Harold J. Sala, Heroes: People Who
Made a Difference in Our World**

**Acknowledge and take to heart this day
that the Lord is God in heaven above and
on the earth below. There is no other.**
Deuteronomy 4:39, NIV

Dear God,

I believe that you are the God in heaven above, but sometimes it doesn't seem like you are the God on earth, too. There are so many rotten things that happen—really bad things like kids killing other kids, parents hurting children, people starving to death. Do you forget about us down here sometimes? Are you so busy being the God of heaven that you don't have time to be the God of earth?

OK, I know I'm being kind of crazy—after all, I do *know* that you're the God of earth, too. But it's a little hard to tell now and then and so I just rush into thinking negatively. I think I need to be more patient while I learn about how you work. Help me to remember that just because things aren't perfect doesn't mean you aren't still in charge. I only have to think about how much worse the world would be if you weren't here, keeping watch over us. Thank you.

June 21

Isaiah said, "God doesn't count us; he calls
us by name. Arithmetic is not his focus."
Romans 9:27, TM

Lord,
    So often I feel like just a number. I have a
school ID number. I have a driver's license
number. I have a social security number. I
have a savings account number. I have an
employee number. All those numbers can
make me feel more like a faceless robot than
a human being!
    I'm glad that I'm not just a number to
you. I'm glad that you know me by my name.
It helps me to realize how much you must
love me—I want to treat others with the same
kind of respect and honor. It feels good to
know that someone cares about the real me.

June 22

What does the Lord your God ask of you but to fear the Lord your God, to walk in all his ways, to love him, to serve the Lord your God with all your heart and with all your soul, and to observe the Lord's commands and decrees that I am giving you today for your own good?

Deuteronomy 10:12–13, NIV

God,

Your commands, the Ten Commandments, seem so old-fashioned—and so obvious. I'm not saying they aren't great guidelines to live by, but why did you have to spell them all out for us like that? Who doesn't know it's wrong to steal, to lie, to cheat, to murder? Why exactly did you write down such obvious things?

But the funny thing is, if they're so apparent to us, isn't that kind of proof that you're out there? If we all automatically know the difference between right and wrong, that must have come from somewhere or someone, right? You must have given that to us already.

These commandments can't save us from sin—only Christ does that—but keeping these commandments saves us from untold heartache and unwanted consequences. God's commandments bring an order to life. When we put Him first, live honorably with family and others, are content with what we have—in other words, do the very things His laws require—life just works.

—*Bill Hybels,* Engraved on Your Heart: Living the Ten Commandments Day by Day

June 23

Even though on the outside it often looks like things are falling apart on us, on the inside, where God is making new life, not a day goes by without his unfolding grace.

2 Corinthians 4:16, TM

Dear Lord,

There are some people who seem like they have it all together. They look right. They say the right things. They hang with the right people. They wear the right clothes.

I don't feel that way. Sometimes it seems like I'm hanging on, just barely making it through the day and hardly surviving all the little things that come my way.

But inside, God—well, I know you're working on me inside. I know you're teaching me things. I know you're changing me little by little to become the person you intend me to be. I may not look all put together on the outside, but on the inside, where it matters most, I know good things are happening. Thank you.

Childlike faith is not for people who need a little help; it is for people who are desperate, who are at the end of their rope. Faith is for those who are not too proud to wave their arms and admit they are drowning.

—Michael Yaconelli, Dangerous Wonder: the adventure of childlike faith

June 24

But whoever did want [Jesus] who believed he was who he
claimed and would do what he said,
He made to be their true selves, their child-of-God selves.
John 1:11–13, TM

God,

A lot of people today tell me I should be "real." They say I should talk about how I'm feeling. They say I should say whatever is on my mind. They say I should do anything I feel like doing. But to me, that doesn't feel like being "real." That feels like putting on a mask and pretending I'm the person everyone else thinks I should be. Well, that's just not me. That's just not real, OK?

I mean, I don't even know who I really am right now. I feel differently about things on different days. Sometimes I think I know exactly what I want for my future and then I feel totally confused about it. I might think one thing one day and then change my mind the next because of something I've heard or read.

Through it all, though, I do know this about myself—I am your child. No matter what I end up doing, no matter where I end up living, no matter who I spend the rest of my life with, that part of my identity will never change. That's the actual, 100 percent true, "real" me.

The only one who knows the "real" you is the one who made you—God. By getting to know him, you'll get to know yourself.

June 25

**I will lie down and sleep in peace, for you alone,
O Lord, make me dwell in safety.**

Psalm 4:8, NIV

O Christ, Son of the living God,
May your holy angels guard our sleep.
May they watch us as we rest
And hover around our beds.

Let them reveal to us in our dreams
Visions of your glorious truth,
O High Prince of the universe,
O High Priest of the mysteries.

May no dreams disturb our rest
And no nightmares darken our dreams.
May no fears or worries delay
Our willing, prompt repose.

May the virtue of our daily work
Hallow our nightly prayers.
May our sleep be deep and soft,
So our work be fresh and hard.

—a Celtic prayer

June 26

"Ah, Sovereign Lord," I said, "I do not know how to speak;
I am only a child." But the Lord said to me, "Do not say, 'I am
only a child.' You must go to everyone I send you to and say
whatever I command you. Do not be afraid of them, for I am
with you and will rescue you," declares the Lord.

Jeremiah 1:6–8, NIV

God,

I'm afraid to tell others about you. I'm afraid of what
they might say and think. Besides, I'm not any good at it. It
just sounds stupid when I try to explain you and what
you're like and how you make me feel. I'm not ready for
this. Can't you give me more time to get ready, more time
to grow up as a Christian?

If you really have something for me to do (but
please—don't let it be talking!), then help me to get mentally to where I can do it. I'll try to be willing, but I know I'll
be nervous.

I know you're always with me, God, but please be
patient while I gather my courage to share you with others.
I'm trying. I really am. And I know that with your help,
someday I'll be ready. Amen.

*God will not ask you to do more than you are able, but
neither will he let you be content with doing less than you
can. You must always try to grow as a Christian and know
that God is there helping you every step of your journey.*

June 27

> **Hosea said, "I'll call nobodies and make them somebodies; I'll call the unloved and make them beloved. In the place where they yelled out, 'You're nobody!' they're calling you 'God's living children.' "**
>
> **Romans 9:25–26, TM**

Dear Lord,

I guess every person probably feels like a "nobody" at one time or another. And—I hope—most people get to feel like a "somebody" at times, too. It feels good to be noticed by other people. It sounds shallow, but being noticed makes me feel worthy and valued.

At school, there are definitely "somebodies" and "nobodies" all around. It really stinks. Of course, no one wants to be a "nobody." And to tell you the truth, I'm not sure what makes someone a "nobody." Maybe it's the clothes they wear? That they look different? That they're too smart? That they're not smart enough?

I know how bad it feels to think no one notices you, to feel like a nothing. God, help me not to label anyone as a "nobody." Help me to see more deeply than just clothes or looks or labels that other kids put on someone else. Help me to see them through your eyes and realize that every-one is a "somebody" who is loved by you. Amen.

The nicest thing we can do for our heavenly Father, is to be kind to one of His children.
—St. Teresa of Ávila

In my distress I called upon the Lord; to my God
  I cried for help. From his temple he heard my
  voice, and my cry to him reached his ears.
                Psalm 18:6, NRSV

Father,
    I know that the best kind of friend is the kind who lis-
tens. So it makes sense that you listen carefully to all the
prayers you hear. But God, how can you do it? How do you
manage to hear every word from every person?
    There are a lot of times when I feel like no one's listen-
ing to me. My parents sometimes ignore me, or else they
totally miss my point (which is *so* annoying!). And my
friends aren't always there when I completely need to vent
or talk things out. I guess it's impossible for anyone to be a
perfect listener—except for you.
    Thank you for listening to me all the time. Thank you
for always being there. I know I have a lot to thank you for,
but this is something that always means a lot to me. It's so
good to know I can talk to you whenever I need to.

> *God is the only one who hears every word at*
> *every moment from every person in every place.*
> *Even more—he doesn't just hear; he listens.*

June 29

Jesus said, "Enter through the narrow gate; for the gate is wide and the road is easy that leads to destruction, and there are many who take it. For the gate is narrow and the road is hard that leads to life, and there are few who find it."

Matthew 7:13, NRSV

God,

Everywhere I look, people are offering quick results. "Lose 10 pounds in one weekend." "Learn to golf in one easy lesson." "Make big money with one quick phone call." What can I say? We're a country of people looking for a quick fix! It seems like everyone expects to get what they want without putting out much effort.

God, I'll be honest. I do the same thing. I want to get good grades without working too hard. I want a job that pays decent money but doesn't require much effort. I want things to be smooth with my family without spending much time working on it. And I want my relationship with you to be strong even when I'm not giving it much thought.

I admire people with character and integrity, those who are willing to put out the effort and time it takes to do something right. They seem to get more out of life. Help me to be that kind of person.

Anything worth doing, having, or being is worth the time, effort, and sacrifice it takes to do it right.

> Just as our bodies have many parts and each part has a
> special function, so it is with Christ's body. We are all
> parts of his one body, and each of us has different work
> to do. And since we are all one body in Christ, we belong
> to each other, and each of us needs all the others.
>
> **Romans 12:4, NLT**

Dear God,

It's hard not to compare myself to other people. I always find myself noticing the people who are better-looking than I am, who are more talented, more athletic, more confident. . . more *everything*. And after looking at them for awhile, I find myself wishing I could be more like them.

God, you made me the way I am. Help me to remember that. And help me to be content with this wonderful creation of a body that you made just for me. I know that I have an important role in life, a role that no one else can fill. I don't want to spend my whole life trying or wishing to be someone different. Thank you for making me unique and for loving me. Amen.

Being content with who you are is one of the most worthwhile accomplishments in life. It's also one of the hardest. Don't give up.

My Thoughts & Prayers

What's been on your mind (and heart) this month? Have you had any big answers to prayer? What's your most important prayer request? Use this space to keep track of all that's been going on.

_____

_____

_____

_____

_____

_____

_____

_____

_____

_____

_____

_____

_____

_____

_____

_____

_____

_____

July 1

We are confident of all this because of our great trust in God through Christ. It is not that we think we can do anything of lasting value by ourselves. Our only power and success come from God.

2 Corinthians 3:4–5, NLT

God, I know that my life matters to you. I believe that you are proud of me when I work hard to accomplish something. I know that you care about my feelings when I fail or fall short of a goal. I have confidence that I am important to you—not because of how well I perform, but because of how much you love me. And so I have confidence in myself—not because of how well I perform, but because of how much you love me.

God, thank you so much for loving and believing in me. You and your love are what drive me and encourage me and inspire me and give me confidence. What blessings! Thank you.

Confidence that is born out of pride will crumble. Confidence that is born out of love will only grow.

July 2

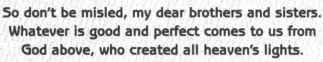

> So don't be misled, my dear brothers and sisters.
> Whatever is good and perfect comes to us from
> God above, who created all heaven's lights.
>
> *James 1:16–17, NLT*

Father,

Today, I just want to thank you for all the cool stuff you've given me. I spend so much time wanting other things that I don't usually take the time to thank you for what I do have. I'm going through the things I own that I really like. You've given me really great stuff that means a lot to me.

I know you've given me gifts that are way more important than physical possessions—and I'm grateful for those, too. But today, I just wanted to say thanks for the stuff. Help me to honor you with the things you let me have. Help me never to put them above you—just to remember that you're ultimately the one who gives them to me.

People, places and things are the
gifts of life, not the Source of life.

—Gary Smalley with John Trent,
Love Is a Decision

July 3

For this reason, a man will leave his father and
mother and be united to his wife, and the two will
become one flesh. This is a profound mystery—
but I am talking about Christ and the church.
Ephesians 5:31–32, NIV

Lord,

I don't know for sure that I'm going to get married
someday—but I might. If so, please help my future spouse
to know your love right now. Help that person to trust in
you and learn how to love. Prepare us both to be good
partners and mates.

If I'm going to get married, Father, I pray that you'll
help my future mate to learn life's important lessons.
Please provide good teachers and mentors and prevent
both of us from chasing things that don't matter. I want to
have a marriage that is strong and lasting and romantic and
that honors you, Father. Please prepare us both for that.

*In marriage, being the right person is as
important as finding the right person.*
—Wilbert Donald Gough

July 4

> I say this for your own benefit, not to put any
> restraint upon you, but to promote good order
> and unhindered devotion to the Lord.
>
> *1 Corinthians 7:35, NRSV*

God,

I don't know how I'm supposed to have plenty of time to spend with you when I don't even have plenty of time to spend with my family or friends or to do all the things I have to do. It feels like I'm always two steps behind, always rushing from one thing to the next, always cramming in last-minute details.

I wish I had more time for everything, especially relaxing and enjoying life. And I wish I had more time to spend with you. I need to make it a priority—if I don't, then it's too easy to get pushed aside and forgotten.

Forgive me for often making you the last thing on my list of priorities. I want you to be the first thing. I know that's how it should be. Amen.

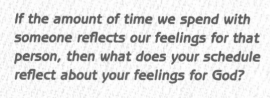

If the amount of time we spend with someone reflects our feelings for that person, then what does your schedule reflect about your feelings for God?

July 5

You can readily recall, can't you, how at one time the more you did just what you felt like doing—not caring about others, not caring about God—the worse your life became and the less freedom you had? And how much different is it now as you live in God's freedom, your lives healed and expansive in holiness?
Romans 6:19–20, TM

God,

    Freedom is a big deal. Everyone wants to be free to follow their own dreams. Everyone wants to be free from silly rules and regulations. Everyone wants to be free to come and go as they please.

    If everyone lived that kind of freedom, the world would be in worse shape than it is now. It's true what they say— that boundaries don't really enslave you, they free you. Strange, but true. I can't imagine a football or basketball game without boundaries. It wouldn't be freedom—it would be chaos.

    Thank you for giving me guidelines that free me from living in the chaos of a world without boundaries. Amen.

If freedom meant being able to do whatever I please, then I would end up being a slave to myself.

July 6

Don't become so well-adjusted to your culture that you fit into it without even thinking. Instead, fix your attention on God. You'll be changed from the inside out.
Romans 12:2, TM

Jesus,

There are times when I don't really act or live any differently than people who don't follow you. And that's not really a good thing. I know then that I've started buying into the whole "me-first" lifestyle I see all around me. I'll do really stupid things like believe that one more new outfit will make me happier or think my success in life is measured by my grades or number of friends.

I want to live in the world without feeling completely out of place, and I don't think you expect me to lock myself in my room and never come out so that I'm not ruined by what's around me. Help me not to have my head so far in the clouds that I'm no earthly good to you.

I know there's a balance out there somewhere. Please help me to realize that there's a difference between living in the world and living *for* the world. Amen.

We are Christians who must live in this world that God has created for us. The trick is to live in the world without learning to love it more than you love God.

**Fix your thoughts on what is true and
good and right. Think about things that
are pure and lovely, and dwell on the
fine, good things in others.**
Philippians 4:8, TLB

My Father,

I'm learning more and more about how to control my words and my actions. It's not easy, but I'm working on it. But how do I control my thoughts? I don't consciously choose what I'm going to think about—it's just suddenly there in my mind. Sometimes it's a good thought. But you and I both know that sometimes it's not.

There *must* be ways that I can control my thoughts. Like maybe I need to choose the right situations to be in or I need to be careful about what I see and hear. For example, I could walk away from a conversation that's heading in a wrong direction. Maybe if I make a point of thinking about positive things, it will help crowd out the other things that aren't so positive. Then my thoughts will have to become better because there's less negative stuff in my head to feed off of.

Help me to figure this out, God, because I know that my thoughts are a reflection of who I am.

July 8

**So, whether you eat or drink or whatever you do,
do everything for the glory of God.**
1 Corinthians 10:31, NRSV

God,

 I know that some people watch how I live. They know I follow you, and so they keep a close eye on how I talk, how I treat others, how I act outside of school. And God—though I'm not perfect—I really try to live the way I think you want me to.

 But I've never thought about my schoolwork that way. I never considered classes or homework or tests to be things that would matter to you or that other people would notice. I'm not a great student. But because I know you want me to work hard at whatever I'm doing, I'll give my schoolwork the attention I should—not because I want to be a straight-A student (though that would be nice!), but because I love you.

*Every single part of every single day—
even studying—can be an act of love
for God.*

July 9

**A gossip goes around revealing
secrets, but those who are
trustworthy can keep a confidence.**
Proverbs 11:13, NLT

Father,

Every once in a while, some bit of gossip comes my way that's really interesting and I start aching to tell someone else about it. I want to be the one who knows things. It makes me feel special and important. I want to pass on the news to my friends, so we can all talk about it.

But, Father, I know you don't like that. For one thing, I don't always know if the gossip is true. And even if it is, I'm not helping the person I'm talking to others about. You know I've been hurt by gossip before—so why do I want to pass stuff like that on?

Help me to be wise, Father, about what I listen to and what information I tell others.

*Gossip is an evil thing by nature, she's a light
weight to lift up, oh very easy, but heavy to carry,
and hard to put down again.*
—Hesiod

July 10

My steps have held fast to your paths;
my feet have not slipped.

Psalm 17:5, NIV

God,

    The daily grind of trying to live the right way can be so exhausting, especially when I find myself surrounded by a lot of people who don't follow you. There's so much pressure to do this, to try that, to experiment with this. . . . Saying no isn't always easy.

    I know I sound kind of down right now, God, but it just overwhelms me at times. Please help me to remember that I don't have to live my whole life in one day. I have to think of it in small steps. I just need to follow you one minute at a time, one hour at a time, one day at a time. I know it would help if I could just keep that in mind. No matter what, I'm not giving up, God. You're too important to me.

The best way to ensure a good future is to live your life in the moment—little by little, step by step.

A heart at peace gives life to the body,
    but envy rots the bones.
        Proverbs 14:30, NIV

O God, who gives to your children liberally, preserve us from all envy at the good of our neighbor and from every form of jealousy.

Teach us to rejoice in what others have and we have not, to delight in what they achieve and we cannot accomplish, to be glad in all that they enjoy and we do not partake of; and so fill us daily more completely with love, through our Savior Jesus Christ.

—*William Knight*

July 12

> So God created man in his own image,
> in the image of God he created him;
> male and female he created them.
>
> *Genesis 1:27, NIV*

God,

    I don't like myself sometimes. I don't like my hair or my clothes or my body. Compared to me, some people seem so graceful and smart and in charge of themselves. Why can't I be like that? Why does it sometimes feel like everything I do is lame and pointless and geeky and awkward?

    I know, I know, I'm exaggerating. But it really does seem that way once in a while. When I start to get down on myself like that, help me to remember that it isn't true, that you love me, and that you've made me in your image. Just like you, I have a mind, a will, and emotions. And because you made me that way, you must have something planned for my life.

    Thank you for how you've made me—even if I don't always appreciate it yet.

Despite how bad we might sometimes feel about our appearances, there could be nothing more beautiful than God's image reflected in all of us.

July 13

Then [Jesus] said to the crowd, "If any of you wants to be my follower, you must put aside your selfish ambition, shoulder your cross daily, and follow me. If you try to keep your life for yourself, you will lose it. But if you give up your life for me, you will find true life."

Luke 9:23–24, NLT

Lord, make me an instrument of your peace. Where there is hatred, let me sow love; where there is injury, pardon; where there is doubt, faith; where there is despair, hope; where there is darkness, light; where there is sadness, joy.

O divine Master, grant that I may not so much seek to be consoled, as to console; to be understood, as to understand; to be loved, as to love. For it is in giving that we receive; it is in pardoning that we are pardoned; and it is in dying that we are born to eternal life.

—*St. Francis of Assisi*

It's so hard to grasp—our greatest rewards in heaven and on earth come from our ability to be selfless. To win the prize, we've got to help everyone get to the finish line ahead of us.

July 14

So teach us to count our days
that we may gain a wise heart.
Psalm 90:12, NRSV

Father,
    I know I'll be with you forever in heaven, but I want my time on earth to count for something. So many people I know seem to be just getting by or chasing fun and good times. I don't want to do that. I want to spend my life completely for you. I want every day I live to count. I want you to use me whenever you can.
    Please, Father, give me the wisdom to know how to spend all my time and energy. Give me the courage not to keep any of it from you, but to let you have it all. Help me to catch on quickly when I'm spending my time on something worthless so I can stop and move on to something better. Help me to seize every day for you.

No one ever regrets using time wisely. No one ever wishes he or she wouldn't have lived a day for God.

Don't be impressed with charisma; look for character.
Matthew 7:20, TM

God,

I hate the term "role model." A role model just sounds so corny. But I have to admit there are certain celebrities that I sort of admire and respect. Lately, I've been disappointed with some of those people. Movie stars, musicians, and even politicians aren't always who they claim to be. They do things that I can't respect at all. I don't understand. These people seem to have everything—fame, talent, money, success—and yet they still seem totally miserable.

Image seems to matter a lot to people. But you say image isn't important. It's character—what's inside a person—that really matters. I really want to be a person of character. And I want to start looking up to people who aren't just all image but who have character, too. Please help me to work on that, God.

You can have all the fame and fortune in the world,
but being a person of honor, integrity, and character
is still the greatest accomplishment of all.

July 16

In him was life, and that life was the light
of men. The light shines in the darkness,
but the darkness has not understood it.
John 1:4–5, NIV

May I follow a life of compassion in
pity for the suffering of all living things.
Teach me to live with reverence for life
everywhere, to treat life as sacred, and
respect all that breathes. O Father, I
grope amid the shadows of doubt and
fear, but I long to advance toward the
light. Help me to fling my life like a
flaming firebrand into the gathering
darkness of the world.

—*Albert Schweitzer*

*It takes only one tiny flame, one small
ray, or one seemingly insignificant
flash to push away the darkness and
introduce the light. Try always to be a
carrier of light.*

When words are many, sin is not absent,
   but he who holds his tongue is wise.
                    Proverbs 10:19, NIV

God,

   I'm coming to you to ask for wisdom about a very specific subject—when to talk and when to keep my mouth shut. I often seem to do exactly the opposite of what I should when it comes to talking. I say the wrong thing at the wrong time. Or I make the mistake of not saying anything when I should have said something.

   God, please help my words to honor you. Help me not to talk just because there's an awkward silence or because I like talking. And when I should speak, please give me the wisdom to know what to say and how to say it. Let my words be used for good—not used to hurt anyone. Amen.

Better to remain silent
and be thought a fool
than to speak out and
remove all doubt.
              —Abraham Lincoln

July 18

Now what I am commanding you today is not too difficult for you or beyond your reach. It is not up in heaven, so that you have to ask, "Who will ascend into heaven to get it and proclaim it to us so we may obey it?" Nor is it beyond the sea, so that you have to ask, "Who will cross the sea to get it and proclaim it to us so we may obey it?" No, the word is very near you; it is in your mouth and in your heart so you may obey it.

Deuteronomy 30:11–14, NIV

Dear Lord,
    It's pretty amazing to think that you actually spoke to people and told them how to live. It's nice that there is no magic place I have to go or a code I have to memorize to know your secret to living real life. It's all there in the Bible. In fact, a lot of it is in my heart and in my conscience. I can sense your presence, and I can often feel you nudging me this way or that when I'm making decisions.
    God, thank you for always being so available to me. It would be impossible to follow and love you if you were cloaked in darkness and the unknown. Even though I don't totally understand you, I certainly understand enough to follow you. Thanks.

No one can complain that it's too difficult to figure out God's plan for life. God has spelled it out plainly in the Bible.

July 19

God said to Moses, "I Am Who I Am."
This is what you are to say to the
Israelites: "I Am has sent me to you."
Exodus 3:14, NIV

God,

"I Am." What a strange name for you. What does that mean anyway? I wonder if you used that name because you are too big and mysterious and incomprehensible for a human being to understand. I sure don't understand you—but I do feel like I'm starting to know you. I know that you are loving. I know that you are patient. I know that you are kind and good and faithful. I also know that you are complicated and complex. You are more powerful than anything I can imagine.

The more I think about it, the more "I Am" seems to fit you. You Are. Period. That seems to cover it all.

I can't believe that someone who is "I Am" would care about me. Thank you.

God is all-knowing. God is all-powerful. God is all-present. What better name could there be for him than simply "I Am."

July 20

Say the welcoming word to God—"Jesus is my Master"—
embracing, body and soul, God's work of doing in us what he
did in raising Jesus from the dead. That's it. You're not "doing"
anything; you're simply calling out to God, trusting him to do it
for you. That's salvation. With your whole being you embrace
God setting things right, and then you say it, right out loud:
"God has set everything right between him and me!"

Romans 10:9, TM

Father,

How is this possible? How can you make me such a
great offer of life without asking for anything in return?

It's sort of hard not to be suspicious. Nothing is free in
today's world—not even friendship. There's always some
string attached, some hidden cost, some payment that
must be made.

So why is it different with you? You could demand any
price for the friendship that you offer. After all, you're God.
Knowing you personally is a priceless thing.

Maybe that's it—because you are God, there is no way
I could ever pay you enough to have a friendship with you.
And so you offer it to me freely. I don't know what to say—
please help me to never take this gift for granted.

*The things that are worth the most can
never have a price attached to them.*

Since the Master honors you with a body, honor him with your body! Or didn't you realize that your body is a sacred place, the place of the Holy Spirit? Don't you see that you can't live however you please, squandering what God paid such a high price for? The physical part of you is not some piece of property belonging to the spiritual part of you. God owns the whole works. So let people see God in and through your body.

1 Corinthians 6:13, 19–20, TM

Dear God,

Sometimes in my relationship with you I get so caught up in things like praying, loving others, trying to be kind and encouraging—using my mind and my words in the right way—that I forget about honoring you with my body. Since you created me and gave me this body, I want to take care of it. That means—as bogus as it can sometimes be—eating right, exercising, and getting enough sleep. It probably also means I should wear clothes that don't make too much of a spectacle of my body.

And when I think about it, honoring my body also means keeping myself pure until I'm married. I think that's the hardest one of all! I'm really curious, and there are so many messages about sex all over the movies, on television, in magazines, and everywhere.

God, help me take care of my body in a way that honors you and respects myself. I know that you know this can be a tough thing to always do. Please help me out. I don't want to be obsessed with my body; I just want to be wise about the choices I make that will affect it.

July 22

He has given me a new song
to sing, a hymn of praise to our God.
Many will see what he has done and be
astounded. They will put their
trust in the Lord.

Psalm 40:3, NLT

All praise to Him who now hath turned
My fears to joys, my sighs to song,
My tears to smiles, my sad to glad. Amen.

—*Anne Bradstreet*

When we trust in God, it doesn't change him. But it begins to change us from the inside out. Knowing that he loves us—and that he's our hope—gives us every reason to be at peace, to be content, to sing out.

**Stay away from the love of money;
be satisfied with what you have. For
God has said, "I will never, *never*
fail you nor forsake you."**
Hebrews 13:5, TLB

Jesus,

I've heard someone say that money is the root of all evil. Maybe that's true, but people need money to survive so I don't really understand how it can be all bad. But if I look at what you taught, I realize that the *love* of money is the root of all evil. I can believe that.

Everything costs money. Going to a movie. Going out to eat. Going to a concert. It's almost impossible to do something for free, unless I just stay at home. And the things I want—clothes, a car, CDs—all cost money. I never have as much money as I wish I did. There's always one more thing I wish I could afford.

It's that sort of thinking that worries me. I don't want to get obsessed with money. It can buy me things, but I know it can't buy me contentment and happiness. I don't want my life to revolve around money—I want it to revolve around you and the people I care about.

Money definitely has its uses, but it also has its problems. Too often, money is just a crutch for people who are looking for real purpose in life.

July 24

Jesus said, "The thief comes only to steal and kill and destroy.
I came that they may have life, and have it abundantly."
John 10:10, NRSV

O Christ, you came so that we might
    have life and have it
more abundantly,
grant us power in our love,
strength in our humility,
purity in our zeal,
kindness in our laughter,
and your peace in our hearts at all times.
    —*J. L. Cowie*, Worship Now

*Jesus gives the ability to live life to the fullest, but he left it
up to us. We can choose lives of boredom and dullness just by
ignoring his commands.*

> **Put me on trial, Lord, and cross-examine me. Test my motives and affections. For I am constantly aware of your unfailing love, and I have lived according to your truth.**
> *Psalm 26:2–3, NLT*

God,

It's not easy to be totally open and honest with other people. It's easier to keep certain things private, deep inside of myself. So being totally open and honest with myself should be easy—right? Then why isn't it?

It's especially hard for me to know what my real motives are. For example, am I nice to certain people because it's the right thing to do—or just because I hope someone will notice and be impressed with my goodness? When I offer to help a popular kid with homework, is it because it's the right thing to do—or because I'm hoping it will help my chances of getting included in a certain crowd?

Sometimes I don't know. But you do. Please, God, test my motives to make sure they're right. And if they're not, then help give me a new attitude so I can try again.

Doing right things for the wrong reasons results in hollow relationships and empty hearts.

July 26

The Lord said, "The Lord doesn't make decisions the way you do! People judge by outward appearance, but the Lord looks at a person's thoughts and intentions."
1 Samuel 16:7, NLT

Lord,

I'm afraid I'm just not good-looking. Why can't I look more like the people on TV or in magazines—or even the popular kids at school? My face, my body—I just don't think there's any way that I'll ever be thought of as great-looking or attractive. And I'm afraid that will keep me from ever finding someone who will want to go out with me.

I know it sounds shallow, but that's how I feel. I know you've made me to be so much more than just how I look. But I still want people to like how I look—especially people that I want to date. Help me to know how to think about my looks. Help me to care as much about who I am on the inside as on the outside. And help me to look as good as I can, if that's OK with you, God.

Anyone who only likes you just for your looks won't like you for very long. Attraction based on looks alone just doesn't last.

Do not think of yourself more highly than you ought, but rather think of yourself with sober judgment, in accordance with the measure of faith God has given you.
Romans 12:3, NIV

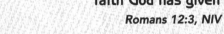

Father,

    I want to thank you for the person you've made me to be—for the person you're still making me. Sometimes, I take too much credit for who I am, thinking I'm pretty cool because I can do something in a certain way. But I know anything good about me has come from you. My body, my mind, and my abilities are all gifts from you. Thank you.

    Other times, Lord, I put you down by putting myself down. I make mean jokes about the way I look or talk or the trouble I have doing something that seems so easy for others. I start to think that I'm a mistake. What an insult to the God who created me! You don't make mistakes.

    Help me, God, to think about myself the right way—and to always thank you for who you've created me to be.

The line between pride and humility is honesty. And the truth is that we are all simply God's creatures—not self-made creators.

Praise the Lord, everything he has created, everywhere in his kingdom. As for me—I, too, will praise the Lord.
Psalm 103:22, NLT

All you big things bless the Lord
Mount Kilimanjaro and Lake Victoria
The Rift Valley and the Serengeti Plain
Fat baobabs and shady mango trees
All eucalyptus and tamarind trees
Bless the Lord
Praise and extol him for ever and ever.
All you tiny things bless the Lord
Busy black ants and hopping fleas
Wriggling tadpoles and mosquito larvae
Flying locusts and water drops
Pollen dust and tsetse flies
Millet seeds and dried dagga
Bless the Lord
Praise and extol him for ever and ever.
—an African canticle

Nothing shows God's glory as well as his creation.

Don't just pretend that you love others. Really love them. Hate what is wrong. Stand on the side of the good.
Romans 12:9, NLT

Dear God,

I want to be a sincere person. I don't want to act one way, but feel another way on the inside.

That's why I'm confused. You tell me to love everyone . . . even if they're my enemies. So if I feel unloving toward them on the inside, you still want me to act loving toward them on the outside. But you also tell me not to fake it. How can I possibly do both?

Teach me how to love others sincerely. And when I'm not feeling the same way, keep me from loving with shallow or wrong motives. I want to follow your lead. I want to love others because of you, not just to try to get something for myself.

We don't always feel our way into good behavior; rather, we behave our way into good feeling.
—**Higher Ground: Taking Faith to the Edge!**

July 30

But if you are unwilling to serve the Lord, then choose today whom you will serve. . . . But as for me and my family, we will serve the Lord.
Joshua 24:15, NLT

Lord Jesus Christ,
I praise and thank you for my parents
and my brothers and sisters,
whom you have given me to cherish.
Surround them with your tender loving care,
teach them to love and serve one another in
    true affection
and to look to you in all their needs.
I place them all in your care,
knowing that your love for them is greater than
    my own.
keep us close to one another in this life
and conduct us at last to our true heavenly home.
Blessed be God for ever. Amen.
                                    —*Michael Buckley*

July 31

For you have been called to live in freedom—not freedom to satisfy your sinful nature, but freedom to serve one another in love. For the whole law can be summed up in this one command: "Love your neighbor as yourself."
Galatians 5:13–14, NLT

God,

I'm realizing that you give freedom a whole new meaning. I've never thought about love and freedom as having much to do with each other. "Love" seemed to be about how I felt and "freedom" seemed to be about living however I wanted to.

Before I really knew you, there were certain people who I could not love. It just was not possible. Really, it wasn't—no matter how hard I thought I tried, my own feelings stopped me from loving them.

With you in my life, though, it's different. Now, my feelings don't control what I do. I finally understand what love truly means. I'm learning how to look at people who I never could have loved before and really love them. You're not forcing me to do it. You're *freeing* me to do something I couldn't before.

Thank you, God. You are amazing! Amen.

My Thoughts & Prayers

What's been on your mind (and heart) this month? Have you had any big answers to prayer? What's your most important prayer request? Use this space to keep track of all that's been going on.

_____

_____

_____

_____

_____

_____

_____

_____

_____

_____

_____

_____

_____

_____

_____

_____

_____

And now, dear brothers and sisters, let me say one more thing as I close this letter. Fix your thoughts on what is true and honorable and right. Think about things that are pure and lovely and admirable. Think about things that are excellent and worthy of praise.

Philippians 4:8, NLT

God,

I just realized something that's so simple I'm surprised that I haven't thought about it before: I can think about whatever I want. I can't always say what I want, and I certainly can't do whatever I want (although it'd be nice if I could!). But no one can keep me from thinking anything.

But that makes me wonder why I think about some of the things that I do. When thoughts come to me, I don't have to hold on to them. So why do I think about things that make me angry? Or grudges? Or things that scare me? Or things that worry me? If I can really think about anything I want, why don't I spend more time thinking about things worth thinking about?

Please remind me to think good thoughts. And if my mind starts to wander, snap me back to what's good and true. I want to think smart.

Every action starts with a thought. Worthless thoughts can lead to lots of worthless actions.

August 2

> Therefore do not worry about tomorrow, for tomorrow will worry about itself. Each day has enough trouble of its own.
>
> *Matthew 6:34, NIV*

Argh! School hasn't even started yet, and I'm already worrying about it. I think I worry because I know I can't control everything that's going to take place. But the good thing is that you already know what this year holds, and you're on my side. Whatever happens, God, please help me to deal with it. Whatever doesn't happen—help me with that too, please.

Every year, I think that the coming year is going to be the hardest ever; every year, there are new challenges to face. And, every year, there you are and there I am. We get through it together. I survive. Who am I kidding? *You* help me survive. It's good to have you on my team, God. Thanks.

What a wonderful God we have—he is the Father of our Lord
Jesus Christ, the source of every mercy, and the one who so
wonderfully comforts and strengthens us in our hardships and
trials. And why does he do this? So that when others are
troubled, needing our sympathy and encouragement, we can
pass on to them this same help and comfort God has given us.

2 Corinthians 1:3–4, TLB

Jesus,

It would be so nice if you just took away all the troubles in my life—no more disagreements, no more hurt
feelings, no more worries about what lies ahead. I often
wonder why life has to be so hard. What's the purpose?

I already know the answer. When I go through a difficult time, I usually come out stronger in the end. I learn
things about myself, about others, and about you. And I
change just a little bit so that the next time I'm struggling,
I'm a little better able to deal with it.

It also makes me a better friend. When people I know
are going through a hard time, I can understand their feelings better if I've experienced the same thing. Help me to
think of my troubles as a chance to learn and grow so I can
help other people in the same situation. Amen.

Like a true friend, God doesn't step in and try to make
everything smooth and easy. Instead, he says, "I'll walk beside
you every step of the way."

August 4

Jesus said, "I have told you these things, so that in me you
may have peace. In this world you will have trouble. But take
heart! I have overcome the world."

John 16:33, NIV

Lord,

I can't tell you how much I want your peace to fill me
up. I want people to see your peace in my eyes. I want
your peace to change everything about me, starting from
the inside out.

My life isn't peaceful, Lord. You know that. So much
hard stuff happens down here—and I don't expect you to
make all that hard stuff stop. I'm just asking that you'll help
me to live in your peace in the middle of it all. I want to be
so changed by you that I become the peaceful calm in the
middle of the world's storm. Thank you for your peace.

Peace is a daily, a weekly, a monthly process,
gradually changing opinions, slowly eroding old
barriers, quietly building new structures.
—John F. Kennedy

August 5

Be joyful in hope.
Romans 12:12, NIV

Father,

    You are my hope. I'm really starting to learn what that means. For me, anyway, it means that I'm expecting less and less to find satisfaction anywhere else. I'm learning that I won't find meaning in food or clothes or sports or money or sex or cars or music or friends or even earthly love. You are my only hope.

    It's not coming easily, Father. I'm used to looking forward to those things to fill up my life. But they don't seem to be working. The promise that you'll be with me is my hope. That's where my meaning comes from. Help me, Father, to live in that hope.

Hoping in the wrong things steals our joy—because those things don't pay off. We can live in true joy only when we hope in God.

**I will give thanks to the Lord because of
his righteousness and will sing praise to
the name of the Lord Most High.**
Psalm 7:17, NIV

Let us praise and thank God for all great and simple joys;
For the gift of wonder and the joy of discovery;
for the everlasting freshness of experience;

For all that comes to us through sympathy and through
sorrow, and for the joy of work attempted and achieved;
For musicians, poets and craftsmen, and for all who work
in form and color to increase the beauty of life;
For the likeness of Christ in ordinary people, their forbear-
ance, courage and kindness, and for all humble and
obscure lives of service;
Glory be to the Father and to the Son and to the Holy
Ghost ever, world without end.

—*Unknown*

*There is no end to the things we can
thank God for every day.*

August 7

Therefore confess your sins to one another, and pray for one another, so that you may be healed. The prayer of the righteous is powerful and effective.
James 5:16, NRSV

God,

    I try to pray every day. I don't always succeed, but I do try. And I try not to just ask for things—"please give me this and please give me that." I know you're not some kind of Santa Claus sitting up in the sky just waiting to lavish me with whatever toys I might want.

    I think I'm praying with the right attitude. I just want to have a special time to talk with you, to tell you how I'm feeling and ask for help when I'm confused about something. But I'll be honest . . . it doesn't always feel like my prayers accomplish much. I don't know what I'm expecting exactly—not some huge miracle or anything. I guess if I pray as a way of getting to know you better, then my prayers are being answered. And if getting to know you better is helping me to learn how to really live, then my prayers are *really* being answered.

    Thank you for letting me talk to you anytime, anywhere, about anything.

Prayer is the avenue for arriving at God's heart.

August 8

Keep your tongue from evil, and your lips from speaking deceit.
Psalm 34:13, NRSV

God,

When I was young, I'd cringe every time I heard "bad words" that weren't allowed in my house. They sounded so strange to me—harsh, nasty, and mean. It was so weird because I almost lived in two different languages—the one at home and the one in other places.

It's pretty easy to find myself saying things that I never thought I would. When a person hears it all the time, you sort of get used to it and it doesn't bother you so much. You stop noticing it. It doesn't bother you anymore. I can't believe what I sometimes hear at movies—profanity after profanity. But after awhile, I even stop noticing that.

God, I don't believe that you sit up there in heaven waiting to strike down people every time they use foul language. But neither do I believe that a person's language doesn't matter—it *does* matter. A lot. The words that come out of my mouth reflect what is going on in my heart and mind. So, God, help my words reflect a positive, loving attitude. Help me find words that don't offend people. Help me find words that you would approve of. Amen.

While it might not always feel important, words do count. The words you use and the things you say reflect who you are and what you believe.

August 9

Let no evil talk come out of your mouths, but only what is useful for building up, as there is need, so that your words may give grace to those who hear.
Ephesians 4:29, NRSV

Jesus,

I wonder how many words I speak in a single day. Thousands, I'd guess. Maybe more. And I wonder how many of those words are positive, encouraging, helpful, and kind.

Maybe it's not enough to keep myself from using bad language. I should also be trying to make my words positive, make them have a purpose. I could probably say a lot less each day and still accomplish that.

God, help me think before I speak. Show me how to use my words to be helpful. I don't want to spend a lot of energy on words that don't mean anything.

Words are priceless things that should be treasured, not meaningless things that should be tossed about carelessly.

It is obvious what kind of life develops out of trying to
get your own way all the time: repetitive, loveless, cheap sex;
a stinking accumulation of mental and emotional garbage;
frenzied and joyless grabs for happiness...paranoid loneliness;
cutthroat competition; all-consuming-yet-never-satisfied wants;
a brutal temper...uncontrolled and uncontrollable
addictions....I could go on.
Galatians 5:19–21, TM

Dear God,

Is trying to get my own way and living life the way I
want really such a big deal? Does it really result in a totally
messed-up life? I wish it didn't, but deep inside I think it
probably must.

I sometimes think I'd like to call all the shots for
myself without paying any attention to you. But then I look
around me at people who live that way, and I see that your
words are absolutely true. They seem empty, lonely, unfulfilled, and totally lost.

God, when I start trying to take control of things and
ignoring you, please remind me that's not really what I
want. Do something to get my attention so that I stop
before I've done something I might regret.

*God never demands that you give him control
of your life. He just waits patiently until you
realize that there's no other way to live.*

A gentle answer turns away wrath,
but harsh words cause quarrels.
Proverbs 15:1, TLB

My Lord,

I have a problem. I'm not sure what to do when someone gets mad at me. I've got some close relationships, but even those people get angry at me once in a while. Sometimes it's my fault; other times, they're just having a bad day. I understand that anger happens in relationships—I just want to know the best way to respond to it.

Please, God, give me the wisdom to know how to respond when people get mad at me. I don't want to be afraid and run away or let people control me with their anger—but I do want to be a peacemaker. I've seen too many ugly things come from anger. Thank you for helping me with this.

We'll never be successful in our most important relationships until we learn how to drain the anger out of another person's life.
—Gary Smalley with John Trent, Love Is a Decision

August 12

If God is for us, who can be against us? He who did not spare his own Son, but gave him up for us all—how will he not also, along with him, graciously give us all things?
Romans 8:31–32, NIV

Dear God,

I know this sounds kind of crazy, but I feel like everyone's against me right now. It's like they're all out to get me or something. On one level, I know that's not true, but it's just how I feel and I can't seem to help it.

It sort of makes sense that I feel all alone sometimes. I know your enemies don't like to see me follow you too closely. And my family can get so busy when we're all doing our own things and don't have much time for each other. Even my friends can kind of turn on me when they're having a bad day.

But then I always remember that I'm never really alone. So, God, I just want to thank you that you are always on my side because I'm your child. I know I belong to you even when no one else is interested in me. I know you're always there for me, working for me. What else do I really need? Thank you for loving me so much and being so endlessly *with* me.

Even when it feels like the whole world is against you, God is still there with you. You are never alone.

> **When I am afraid, I will trust in you. In God, whose word I praise, in God I trust; I will not be afraid.**
> **Psalm 56:3–4, NIV**

God,

Why is it so easy for me to feel afraid? I'm not talking about that intense someone's-hiding-in-the-closet kind of fear (although I feel that sometimes, too). I'm talking about the kind of fear I feel at school when I hear someone laughing and think they must be talking about me. Or the fear that comes when one of my family members is late getting home, and I start thinking about car accidents and death and being alone. Or that fear that sneaks up on me sometimes that I'm going to waste my life and nothing I ever do will matter.

I know you don't give me those fears, and I don't want them to control me. Help me to trust in you instead of getting caught up in these emotions. If you're really my Father and you really love me—both of which I believe—then I've got nothing at all to be afraid of. The most powerful being in the universe loves and cares for me. Why hold on to fear? Help me to remember that.

August 14

**Be strong and courageous. Do not be
terrified; do not be discouraged, for the Lord
your God will be with you wherever you go.**
Joshua 1:9, NIV

God,

When Joshua was getting ready to lead your people—
finally—into the promised land, you told him to be strong
and courageous because you were going to be with him.
Well, Father, I'm not leading a nation, but I am getting
ready to go back to school, and I feel the need to be
courageous.

Not only am I going to be fighting to do well in my
classes and sports and clubs—I'm going to be fighting to
live for you. With my friends . . . when no one is
looking . . . in front of my teachers, I'm going to need your
courage and strength to stand for you when it would be
easier to do my own thing. Please help me to live coura-
geously this school year, Father.

One man with courage makes a majority.
—*Andrew Jackson*

No temptation has seized you except what is common to man.
And God is faithful; he will not let you be tempted beyond
what you can bear. But when you are tempted, he will also
provide a way out so that you can stand up under it.

1 Corinthians 10:13, NIV

Lord,

It's not a secret to you, I guess, so I might as well talk to you about it: I sometimes want to do things I know are wrong. I've done some of them in the past and, to be honest, I've enjoyed them. It's not that I'm not sure they're wrong. It's not that I'm confused about what you want me to do. You've made it clear in your book.

God, I need your help to beat these temptations. On my own, I'm a goner. I'll just give up and do them. In your power, I've got a chance. Help me to want to keep with your word at least as badly as I want to do these things. Help me want to please you more than anything else. Give me the courage to obey you instead of my own desires.

Every temptation comes with an escape hatch. Don't buy the lie that you've gone too far to turn back. You can turn around at any moment.

August 16

> But you are a forgiving God,
> gracious and compassionate, slow to anger
> and abounding in love.
> *Nehemiah 9:17, NIV*

Is it because you know everything that you are "gracious and compassionate"? I, on the other hand, get mad and want to wreck stuff. I need to show some of your compassion and understanding—at home and with my friends. I'm always getting yelled at, or laughed at, or something else I resent. Help me to do better—to be able to laugh at myself now and then and to realize that everyone makes mistakes.

All I have to do is remember that I'm your child, you love me, and even if today seems like the edge of a crater, you'll get me through it. Moment by moment, we're hanging in there. That's cool.

August 17

Then I saw a new heaven and a new earth, for the first heaven and the first earth had passed away....He will wipe every tear from their eyes. There will be no more death or mourning or crying or pain, for the old order of things has passed away.
Revelations 21:1, 4, NIV

You know, I cried last night for the first time in a long time. I mean, I *really* cried. It started with something little, and before I knew it, there were big gobs of tears running down my face.

In the end, I'd say it felt good to cry. Maybe that's why you gave us tears, so that we could work through sadness or low days and then feel better. Tears can help clean up the little fumbles in our lives.

Thank you that tomorrow is another day, and I'll get a fresh start. Amen.

August 18

And I am convinced that nothing can ever separate
us from his love. Death can't, and life can't. The
angels can't, and the demons can't. Our fears for
today, our worries about tomorrow, and even the
powers of hell can't keep God's love away.
Romans 8:38, NLT

When I do things that are wrong—and *I* know
they're wrong—is it worse than if I didn't know it was
wrong? Is it like in algebra—"sin to the second
power"? And, Lord, I do screw up, don't I? After you
already sent your son to cover my sins, I still manage
to take my shortcomings *so* lightly. (Don't you cringe
when I call my sins "shortcomings"?)

I give my life to you again today, with a new
awareness of who you are and what you've done for
me. Thank you.

Lord,

There's nothing quite like getting a second chance. It's such a great feeling to be able to fix something that's gone wrong—like patching up a friendship or smoothing over an argument with my parents.

But the second chance you've given me—well, there are no words to describe it. It's so awesome to know that all the broken pieces of my past are in your hands. There's no better place for them. When I finally realized that I couldn't fix them myself and decided to give them to you instead, I really did feel changed— complete and whole and put back together. It's an incredible feeling! And I can never give thanks enough for it. You're amazing.

God is always there to help. He's the best at putting broken pieces back together to make a beautiful whole.

How we thank God, who gives us victory over sin and
death through Jesus Christ our Lord!

1 Corinthians 15:57, NLT

I am bending my knee
In the eye of the God
    who created me
In the eye of the Son
    who died for me
In the eye of the Spirit
    who moves me
In love and in desire
For the many gifts
    you have bestowed on me
Each day and night
    each sea and land
Each weather fair
    each calm each wild
Thanks be to you O God

—*J. Philip Newell*, Celtic Prayers from Iona

*True humility includes thanking God for the gifts he's given
us that we could never have come up with on our own.*

I've learned by now to be quite content whatever my circumstances. I'm just as happy with little as with much, with much as with little. I've found the recipe for being happy whether full or hungry, hands full or hands empty. Whatever I have, wherever I am, I can make it through anything in the One who makes me who I am.

Philippians 4:11–13, TM

God,

I wish I knew what my life will be like five or ten years from now. I wonder where I'll be living, what kind of job I'll have, if I'll be married and have a family, if I'll be happy with the way things are.

I have certain dreams about the future and how I'd like it to turn out, but I know there's no guarantee that things will fall into place like I'd planned. God, whatever the future holds, help me to be content with my circumstances. If everything ends up completely different than I'd hoped, I don't want to complain about it and always think, "If only things were different." As long as I'm walking with you, I know I'll end up in the right place.

The will of God is like a flashlight in a dungeon: It doesn't shine around corners or into the next room but it gives you enough light for the next step.

—*Dr. Harold J. Sala*, **Heroes: People Who Made a Difference in Our World**

August 22

**I can't see your faith if you don't have good deeds,
but I will show you my faith through my good deeds.**
James 2:18, NLT

Father,
 I don't have any trouble believing that the
things you say are true. I believe in you and I've
trusted you with my life. Sometimes, though,
I have trouble putting my beliefs into actions.
 God, please help me to make the connection
between what I believe from your word and how
I live my life. Give me the wisdom to apply your
truth to my daily activities. And give me the
courage to live what I know is true when it's hard to
do—or when I just don't want to. I want my whole
life—beliefs and actions—to honor you, God.

*Obedience to God is the
only thing that proves we
believe his word.*

Cast all your anxiety on him because he cares for you.
1 Peter 5:7, NIV

Father,

I'm kind of worried about this school year that's just getting started—I want so many things to go right this year. I'm just going to lay a few of them out there for you, Father—not necessarily to give them all to me, but just to let them go to you.

I want people to like me. I want to be popular. I want to look good. I want to get the grades I need. I want to like my classes. I want to make the teams and clubs I go out for. I want to have a great social life. I don't want to feel awkward and self-conscious all the time.

There. Those are the things on my mind, getting in the way of my just relaxing in you. I give them to you, Father. Help me to let go of them and trust you for this next year of school.

Worry and trust cannot live in the same house. When worry is allowed to come in one door, trust walks out the other door; and worry stays until trust is invited in again, whereupon worry walks out.

—Robert G. LeTourneau

Don't lie to each other, for you have stripped off your old evil nature and all its wicked deeds.
Colossians 3:9, NLT

Dear God,

Not too long ago, I realized someone had told me a lie. It wouldn't hurt so much, except that I believed it. I trusted this person. I never for a second believed that it might be a lie. But now I know it was. And it hurts. I'm feel embarrassed and foolish and betrayed and hurt. And that stinks.

Father, I've lied to people, too—people I love, people I care about. I'm not sure why I do it. Actually, I know exactly why—because it was easier than telling the truth at the time. But, Lord, I don't want to hurt people the way I hurt right now. Help me not to lie. When I'm tempted to fall back into lying, please give me a mental shake and remind me to tell the truth.

Every violation of truth is not only a sort of suicide in the liar, but is a stab at the health of human society.
—Ralph Waldo Emerson

It's a new school year, Lord.
Summer's over.
Thanks for all the great times I had.
Thanks, too, for the summer days
that weren't all that great.

Now it's back to school.
I'd like to think I'm all ready
to make top grades,
star in sports,
and maybe even be a success with the [opposite sex].
You can see right through me, though,
can't you, Lord?

I'm nervous
I'm not as sure of myself
as I want others to believe.
So, Lord, give me the wisdom to ask questions
when I'm not sure what happens next.
Give me the honesty to say, "I don't know,"
when I'm asked a tough question.
Most of all, give me the vision to see a good
  year ahead,
recognizing that a good year is what you want for me,
and that seeing it now, in prayer, ahead of time,
will help make a good year possible. Amen.

—*Dean Nadasdy,* **Tough Days and Talks with God**

August 26

And the Holy Spirit helps us in our distress.
For we don't even know what we should pray for,
nor how we should pray. But the Holy Spirit prays
for us with groanings that cannot be expressed in
words. And the Father who knows all hearts knows
what the Spirit is saying, for the Spirit pleads for
us believers in harmony with God's own will.

Romans 8:26–27, NLT

Father,

I feel things weighing on my heart, deep emotions that I can't quite get into words. I want to tell you about them, but I don't know what to say. I want to open my mouth and just start talking to you, but no words are there. I feel so clumsy when I come to you like this.

Help me to know how to talk to you. Help me to know how to express what I'm feeling and thinking. Help me to know what to ask for, if anything. Thank you that you don't need my words to understand me. Thank you that you know me better than I know myself. Thank you that I am yours even when I can't seem to understand myself.

Not every prayer needs words.

Being confident of this, that [God] who began a good work in you will carry it on to completion until the day of Christ Jesus.

Philippians 1:6, NIV

We must praise your goodness that you have left nothing undone to draw us to yourself. But one thing we ask of you, our God, not to cease to work in our improvement. Let us tend towards you, no matter by what means, and be fruitful in good works, for the sake of Jesus Christ our Lord.

—Ludwig van Beethoven

Why would God go to all the work of saving us if he wasn't also going to keep changing us from the inside out until we are finally like Jesus? Don't get discouraged; he'll get you there.

August 28

When I refused to confess my sin, I was weak and
miserable, and I groaned all day long. Day and night
your hand of discipline was heavy on me. My strength
evaporated like water in the summer heat. Finally, I
confessed all my sins to you and stopped trying to hide
them. I said to myself, "I will confess my rebellion to
the Lord." And you forgave me! All my guilt is gone.

Psalm 32:3–5, NLT

Why do I think I can get away with letting *you* down? I
know my mom or dad will catch me when I try to cover up
something I've done, and yet somehow I pretend to myself
that you won't notice if I don't bring up my mistakes. Well,
you love me, and that means you do notice. And just
because I didn't ask for your forgiveness, that doesn't
mean it didn't happen.

So let's go over this one more time. I sinned. Big time.
OK, REALLY big time. Then I tried to pretend it didn't happen. And when you stabbed my conscience, I still didn't
'fess up. Well, now I'm on my knees. I feel guilty, and it's
not going to go away until you and I work through it. In the
end, please help me to accept your forgiveness.

Jesus Christ is the same yesterday, today, and forever.
Hebrews 13:8, TLB

Lord,

I want to thank you that you don't ever change. Sometimes I feel like there's way too much change going on in my life. Nothing is very stable. You just get used to the freedom of summer and then you've got to head back to school. I'll soon be out of high school, and everything will change forever. And my family is always changing.

So, God, I just wanted you to know how glad I am that you don't change. I know you'll always love me just like you do right now. I know you'll always be God. You're not going to lose your position and have to be replaced. You're a rock, Lord—even when my world is turning over again. I praise you for that.

The ever-changing ocean is easier to deal with when you're anchored to something that cannot be moved.

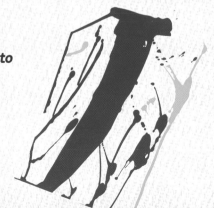

Surely you desire truth in the inner parts; you teach me wisdom in the inmost place.

Psalm 51:6, NIV

O Lord, who is the fountain of all wisdom and learning, you have given me the years of my youth to learn the arts and skills necessary for an honest and holy life. Enlighten my mind, that I may acquire knowledge. Strengthen my memory that I may retain what I have learnt. Govern my heart, that I may always be eager and diligent in my studies. And let your Spirit of truth, judgment and prudence guide my understanding, that I may perceive how everything I learn fits into your holy plan for the world.

—*John Calvin*, The Christian Life

As another school year begins, keep this in mind: Wisdom comes from God above, but God expects you to use your own mind to seek it.

Pray this way for kings and all others who are in authority, so that we can live in peace and quietness, in godliness and dignity.
1 Timothy 2:1–2, NLT

I watched the president today, Lord.
He's always on TV.
Everyone knows him.
People always take his picture.
What he says is important.

Look what You have given to him, God.
He has a fancy house and bodyguards.
He must be very rich.
He never has to mow his yard
or take out the garbage like my dad does.
He will be in history books
for my kids to read about.

But the president needs You, too.
He needs someone to talk to and
who won't tell reporters what he said.
He needs someone to thank
when things go great,
or when nothing goes wrong.
He needs to know that Jesus
is his Savior, just as I do.

Thanks, God, for helping me.
Please help our president too.
—*Eldon Weisheit*, Psalms for Teens, *based on Psalm 21*

My Thoughts & Prayers

What's been on your mind (and heart) this month? Have you had any big answers to prayer? What's your most important prayer request? Use this space to keep track of all that's been going on.

_____

_____

_____

_____

_____

_____

_____

_____

_____

_____

_____

_____

_____

_____

_____

_____

I thank my God every time I remember you.
Philippians 1:3, NIV

God,

    You've given me some great friends. It's not just that I have fun with them—which I obviously do—it's also that they're such cool people. They really seem to care about me and enjoy being around me. I've never really thought about it like this before, but my friends are a great gift from you.

    Thank you for my friends. Thank you for the time we spend together and for the way they like me. Thank you for the fact that we can disagree and still be friends. Thank you for the positive ways we influence each other. I know not everyone has good friends like these. Help me to love them with your kind of love and to be a good friend to each of them.

The best friends are the ones who have seen you be mean, stupid, and ugly—and like you anyway.

September 2

**It's in Christ that we find out who we are and what we
are living for. Long before we first heard of Christ and
got our hopes up, he had his eye on us, had designs on
us for glorious living, part of the overall purpose he is
working out in everything and everyone.**
Ephesians 1:11, TM

God,
   It's such a great feeling to be chosen, whether it's for
a team, for a leadership role, for a special group . . . being
chosen is a great ego-booster. It makes me feel appreciated,
noticed, and worthwhile. Especially in relationships. When
another person chooses me as a friend (OK, it's not really
"choosing," but you get the idea) then I feel great, as
though I were more important than before.
   That's what you did for me, God. You "chose" me, in a
sense, and made an offer of friendship. Me! I can't believe
it sometimes. It makes me feel more appreciated, noticed,
and worthwhile than anything else does.
   Thank you!

*God does not just casually notice
you. He does not just glance your
way. He determinedly chooses you
and then waits for you to realize it
has happened.*

September 3

Stop judging others, and you will not be judged.
For others will treat you as you treat them.
Matthew 7:1, NLT

God,
   Some of the people at school seem to think it's their job to make other kids feel bad about themselves. With their attitudes and their little comments and just the way they look at people and laugh—I wonder if they have any idea how they completely destroy people inside.

   I'll admit I can be that way, too, God. I can make fun of someone for a cheap laugh. I can avoid someone because they don't quite fit in. I don't go around looking to play favorites, but I know I've been mean to some people just because of the way they are.

   I don't want to be that way, God. Help me to be kind instead of mean, especially to the people who can't defend themselves from the school "judgment squad."

The way you treat others has a way of coming back to you. Treat people well, and others tend to treat you well. Treat people unkindly, and you can expect unkindness from others.

God has had it with the proud,
But takes delight in just plain people.
1 Peter 5:5, TM

Jesus,

I don't think pride is always a bad thing. I want to do work that I can be proud of. I don't want to be a person who does things only so-so. I think you expect more of me than that.

Pride is dangerous, though, if I start letting myself have too much of it. Then I start being "stuck up." People like that are hard to be friends with because they're only focused on themselves. I know you want me to be focused on others and on you.

I'm starting to feel OK about being me—just an ordinary, normal, everyday person. I used to think that was the worst thing that could ever happen. But I'm starting to see that ordinary, normal, everyday people can do amazing things, and that's something to be proud of. Keep me from becoming too prideful, God, and instead let me simply be content. Amen.

Those people who accomplish the most extraordinary things live the most ordinary lives.

Listen to advice and accept instruction,
that you may gain wisdom for the future.
Proverbs 19:20, NRSV

O God, teach us to know that failure is
as much a part of life as success—and
whether it shall be evil or good depends
upon the way we meet it—if we face it list-
lessly and daunted, angrily or vengefully,
then indeed is it evil for it spells death. But
if we let our failures stand as guideposts
and as warnings—as beacons and as
guardians—then is honest failure far better
than stolen success, and but a part of that
great training which God gives us to make
us men and women.
                    —W.E.B. DuBois

Our mistakes are not
considered failures and our
failures are not considered
mistakes unless we fail to
learn from them.

> We know very well that we are not set
> right with God by rule keeping but only
> through personal faith in Jesus Christ.
> *Galatians 2:16, TM*

Jesus,

I love you. I believe in you. I want to follow you. But I don't always know how to do that. I'm so used to playing by the rules—rules at school, rules at work, rules at home, rules at church—that it's hard to live any differently. I used to think that if I broke one of your rules, you kept track of it—you know, kind of a score sheet on my behavior. I have a few friends like that. They never let me forget if I've let them down or made a mistake. It almost ruins the relationship because I feel like I'll never be able to measure up.

I'm glad that you don't keep a scorecard on me. I don't think I could live that way. It's so good to know that you love me for *me*, not for my "good things versus bad things" score.

Christianity is not about learning
how to live within the lines;
Christianity is about the joy of
coloring.

—Michael Yaconelli, Dangerous Wonder:
   the adventure of childlike faith

The Lord hates cheating, but he delights in honesty.
Proverbs 11:1, NLT

Lord,

Do you know how much some people at school cheat? I guess you do, don't you? It seems like it's everywhere. The worst part is that everyone thinks it's perfectly normal. Even some of the teachers seem to have given up caring whether students are cheating.

I bring this up, Lord, because it sure would make my life easier just to give in and cheat. I'll admit that the thought does tempt me. If I joined in, I wouldn't have to study quite as much. And it doesn't seem like a big deal.

But, Lord, I do know it is a big deal. I want to do what's right. I want to please you more than I want to have an easier time or get good grades. I want to be honest. Help me not to cheat. Help me to be strong when that temptation comes my way, because it happens a lot.

The worst thing about cheating is that it becomes a pattern for life. It lowers our standards until we're always looking for the easy way—even if it's the wrong way.

September 8

You are to live clean, innocent lives as children of
God in a dark world full of crooked and perverse
people. Let your lives shine brightly before them.
Philippians 2:15, NLT

God,
    If there's only one thing I could do for
the people in my life, it would be to somehow give them a glimpse of how great you
are. I don't know if I'm brave enough to talk
about it with them, so I want to make sure
that I show them through my actions and
my choices.
    I know I won't do a perfect job of it.
I slip up more than I want to. But I'll do my
best, God. I'll try to live in a way that makes
my friends and people that I meet interested
in getting to know you.

*The greatest honor you will ever have
as a Christ-follower is being a Christ-
reflector to others.*

**Many are the afflictions of the righteous,
but the Lord rescues them from them all.**
Psalm 34:19, NRSV

God,

I'll be honest. Sometimes I wish that you'd said, "If you follow me, your heart will never be broken again. If you follow me, no one will ever hurt you again. If you follow me, you'll never experience troubles again."

Certainly that's possible for you. After all, you're God. You can do anything. So why don't you just take away all my problems and make things go smooth and easy?

I'm not sure I know why. After all, I can't figure out a lot of things about you. But I do know this—if I never had my heart broken, if I never had my feelings hurt, if I never lost someone I cared about, if I never had anything go wrong in my life, then I'd never appreciate what you have to offer. In fact, I might completely forget all about you or fool myself into thinking I didn't need you. As long as I'm alive, I'm sure I'll face problems, and I'm sure that every time, I won't understand why I have to go through them. But I'm also sure that you'll be there with me through it all. Thank you.

***God's purpose is to give your life meaning,
not to make your life easy.***

Don't hit back; discover beauty in everyone. If you've got it in you, get along with everybody. Don't insist on getting even; that's not for you to do.

Romans 12:17–19, TM

Lord,

When someone hurts me, I want to strike right back at them. My natural instinct is to give to them what they gave to me. That probably sounds childish—and it probably *is* childish.

I know I can't live life that way. I'd spend every waking minute trying to get revenge, trying to get even. What a horrible way to live. I'd never be happy, joyful, or content. My whole life would be about bad feelings and negativity. I don't need that, and I certainly know you don't want that.

I want to try not to worry about repaying evil for evil. Give me the courage to live differently, to love those people who it seems I shouldn't love at all. I'll never be able to do this on my own, so please help me. Amen.

It's not enough to resist the temptation for revenge; you must also extend the offer of friendship. God always pushes us to go one step further than we think is possible. Find the strength to take that step, and you will be rewarded.

September 11

> God can do anything, you know—far more than you
> could ever imagine or guess or request in your wildest dreams!
> He does it not by pushing us around but by working with us,
> his Spirit deeply and gently within us.
>
> *Ephesians 3:20, TM*

God,

I feel so manipulated sometimes. Teachers at school are trying to turn me into the "right" kind of student. My parents are trying to turn me into a person who agrees with everything they say and do. Even my friends (maybe without realizing it?) are trying to fit me into a certain mold that they think is right for me. It drives me nuts! I'm me! Can't they just accept that? Can't they just appreciate me for me and not try to push me around?

God, thank you for not forcing me into becoming someone I'm not. Thank you for just letting me be who I am and for trying to improve me without trying to change me. I appreciate the fact that you're not always nagging at me and shoving your ideas down my throat. It makes it so much easier. And I truly thank you for that.

God never tries to turn you into someone you're not; he tries to turn you into the someone you really are.

September 12

Whatever you do, work at it with all your heart, as
working for the Lord, not for men, since you know
that you will receive an inheritance from the Lord as
a reward. It is the Lord Christ you are serving.

Colossians 3:23–24, NIV

Father,
    Sometimes, I don't feel like working. Whether
it's homework or chores around the house or my
job, I just don't want to do it. I want to sit. I want
to relax. I want to hang with my friends. Working
seems like such a waste of my time.
    Still, I've got to do it and get it done. Help me
to have a good attitude about my work. Help me
to get over that hump of not getting started or not
paying attention to what I'm doing. I want even my
work to please you, although I'm not sure why you
care. Thank you for the work you've given me to
do and the money and opportunities that come
with it. Thanks, too, that you never stop working
on me.

*Work is a way that we can imitate God by bringing
order to something or creating or using our time and
energy to serve others.*

A friend loves at all times.
Proverbs 17:17, NIV

Father,

I really care about my friends at school. Some of my best moments are when we get together and laugh or go somewhere or just hang out. Thank you for putting these people in my life. They actually make me look forward to going to school—well, most of the time.

That's why I want to be such a good friend to them, Father. I want to be there for them when they need me. I want to encourage them and make them feel better about themselves. I want my life and my actions to point them to you, because I know that's what will make them the happiest. In short, Father, I want to love them with the kind of love you've given to me. Please help me do that.

Your friends have more influence on your life right now than any other group of people. That also means you have the power to influence your friends.

September 14

> The crucible for silver and the furnace for gold,
> but man is tested by the praise he receives.
> **Proverbs 27:21, NIV**

Lord,

You know I try hard to do well. And I think I do a good job in many areas of my life—especially one or two. I hope it's OK to want people to notice, Lord, when I do well at something. I want them to notice and tell me how great I'm doing. It makes me feel good, and I don't think that's a bad thing always. Please help me not to want that *too* much, though.

I also ask, Lord, that you'll help me to know what to say or do when people praise me for something. Help me not to get proud or arrogant. Help me to be able to give the praise to you and to give encouragement back to the people who praise me. And, Lord, help me to be humble enough not to *expect* others to give me praise.

Praise makes good men better and
bad men worse.
　　　—Thomas Fuller, M.D.

September 15

*Such things were written in the Scriptures long ago
to teach us. They give us hope and encouragement as
we wait patiently for God's promises.*

Romans 15:4, NLT

God,

It isn't always easy to sit down and read the Bible. I
have so much other stuff I need to read for school. And
there's always a stack of magazines that I want to look at.
And there's always the Internet sitting there waiting to be
surfed. The Bible just doesn't seem like the most interesting thing around me. Especially since it's so old and talks
about things that don't have anything to do with me.

As I get older, though, I'm trying to read it with a different attitude, and it makes a big difference. If I open the
cover and remember that you wrote those words for *me*,
then it seems to make more sense.

God, thank you for giving me a book that tells me so
much about you, that actually tells me so much about
myself, too. Help me to understand what I read so that it
changes the way I live.

*The Scriptures were given not to increase our knowledge, but
to change our lives.*

—D. L. Moody

September 16

**If you keep your mouth shut,
you will stay out of trouble.**
Proverbs 21:23, NLT

Lord,

I need help with something. I need to develop the skill of keeping my mouth closed. I just need to learn when to shut up. I know I'm in trouble when I start talking to fill dead air. Or when I say something just because I want people to pay attention to me. Or when I open my mouth because I think I'm supposed to have an opinion on something even though I don't know what that opinion is yet.

I really want the wisdom not to talk when I shouldn't. I don't want to hurt people with my words. I don't want to gossip. I don't want to make myself (or you) look stupid by what I say. Help me to speak only when I have something worthwhile to say.

Let thy speech be better than silence, or be silent.
—Dionysius the Elder

Father,

I've done a lot of things I'm sure didn't make you very happy. But there's one I really feel terrible about. I can't seem to get past it. I just want you to know again that I'm really sorry. I was wrong. I shouldn't have done it. I knew even then it was wrong, and I did it anyway. What a waste of my time and yours.

Father, I know I'm your child because I've trusted in Jesus to save me. I know you forgave my sins back then. Thank you for forgiving me both then and now. Give me the strength (and the desire) not to do things that are wrong. I want to please you with my whole life. Amen.

Sin hurts us, because it forces us away from God and out on our own. Fortunately, he is always waiting with open arms for us to come back to him.

September 18

Turn me away from wanting any other plan
than yours. Revive my heart toward you.
Psalm 119:37, TLB

Father, I have a weird relationship with television. I love it and I hate it. I love it when it makes me laugh or makes me think—but I hate how it almost always leaves me feeling empty. Isn't that strange? I can spend so much time with something but it doesn't fill me up at all. I hate how many of my hours it eats up and all the meaningless (and sometimes awful or just plain stupid) images and sounds I've absorbed from it.

I know this sounds kind of corny, but I also worry about what it's doing to our society. Everyone I know watches TV, so I know that we're all seeing things we shouldn't and wasting time that could be used for more important things.

But that doesn't mean I don't like watching TV. I still think it's great a lot of times. After a long day, I love to come home and turn it on and not think about anything. I can laugh and cry and learn and hope. You see how mixed-up I am about it? Please give me wisdom to know how to think about TV—and the self-control to turn it off when I should.

[Television] is a medium of entertainment which permits millions of people to listen to the same joke at the same time, and yet remain lonesome.

—T. S. Eliot

*Of making many books there is no end, and
much study is a weariness of the flesh.*
Ecclesiastes 12:12, NRSV

God,

I hate homework. I could list 38 million things
I'd rather do. But eventually it has to be done, and
I'm stuck with the book open and the papers in
front of me and . . . it's just *so* bogus. Why can't I
just do what I want to?

Help me to see the reason for it. Help me to
choose to give thanks for what I'm learning instead
of complaining about "having" to learn. Help me to
be patient. Help me not to keep putting this stuff
off until there's so much I can't bear to even think
about it—let alone start working on it.

*When even the thought of homework brings
you down, remember this: If you had a
piece of knowledge for every time you
avoided homework, you'd be a grade-A
scholar. Now think of what a genius you'd
be if you just did the homework!*

**God takes particular pleasure in acts of worship—
a different kind of "sacrifice"—that take place in
kitchen and workplace and on the streets.**
Hebrews 13:16, TM

God,

Can you add "school" to that list of places? It's where I spend almost all my time, and if I'm going to do things for you, it will have to happen there.

I used to think that I could only worship you while I was sitting in church or praying. But I think that when I try to be kind to people at school, that's worship. And when I hold my tongue instead of spreading the latest rumor, that's worship. And when I work hard to get my assignments as good as they can be, that's worship.

Thank you for giving my daily life meaning. Even if school seems meaningless to me (and sometimes it does) at least I know that how I live my life at school has purpose. Amen.

*The best place to
serve God is right
where you are.*

September 21

Be still before the Lord, and wait patiently for him.
Psalm 37:7, NRSV

God,

My life is almost never quiet or still. There's always noise and busy-ness all around me—at school, at home, with friends. In fact, I can't remember the last time I sat and just enjoyed the peace and quiet. Actually, I'm so used to sound and activity that sitting in silence sort of makes me feel strange.

I wonder if I'm missing something with all of this chaos distracting me. I don't get to listen to myself think often, let alone listen for you. Your voice is usually drowned out by something or someone (or a whole lot of them). I wonder what I'd hear if I sat quietly and listened for you. I don't mean that I think I'd hear a voice or anything. But I think I'd hear the sound of trees. The sound of air stirring around me. The sound of nature. The sound of my own heartbeat. The sound of silence.

It'd be nice to spend that quiet time with you, God. Help me find a time and a place where I can be silent with you. I want to experience that so I can see what you have to say to me. I'm ready to listen. Amen.

Prayer isn't so much about you talking to God as it is about you listening to God.

September 22

May he grant you your heart's desire and fulfill all your plans.
Psalm 20:4, TLB

Father,

I've got a lot of things going on right now that I need to do well. School's starting to get tough. My clubs and teams are starting up. And I have to fit work and family and friends into all of that! I don't want to drop any of the balls that I'm juggling. I think maybe everything is going to work out, but I sure don't want to try it on my own just to see if I can handle it all. I've done that before. Even when things go OK, it doesn't feel right.

I want your help with these things I have to do. I want to do them in your power, not my own. I want them to matter and to make you happy. Please give me your strength and courage and patience to do these things in the best way I can. Help me to trust you with the results and to be satisfied with whatever happens because I know I did the best I could.

Success is more than just accomplishing the goal—it's getting there in the right way and for the right reasons.

Father,

So many people need to know you. I can think of dozens of people whose lives would totally improve if they had a relationship with you through Jesus. Please, Father, lead those people into knowing you like I do. Help them to see their need for you—and then to let them find you.

And, God, I ask that you'll help me represent you well to everyone. I want them to see you in me. I want them to know just by watching me what a difference you've made in my life. Help me to lead people to you.

Sometimes being a good follower of Christ is the best way to help lead others into his welcoming arms.

The disciples went and woke him, saying, "Master, Master, we're going to drown!" He got up and rebuked the wind and the raging waters; the storm subsided, and all was calm.

Luke 8:24, NIV

Lord,

I read in the Bible about your power over the storm when you were in that boat on the Sea of Galilee with your disciples. They were experienced fishermen, used to being on the water—and they were scared. That must have been some storm. But you were more powerful, Lord. You stopped it with just one word.

I praise you, Lord, for being more powerful than the weather. I've been in some pretty strong storms—and I've seen stronger ones on TV: hurricanes, tornadoes, floods. They can wipe out whole towns. But you're stronger than all of them, Lord. Thank you for your power.

God is greater even than nature—because he created nature.

"Where is your faith?" [Jesus] asked his disciples. In fear and amazement they asked one another, "Who is this? He commands even the winds and the water, and they obey him."
Luke 8:25, NIV

Lord,

Yesterday, I praised you for being stronger than hurricanes, tornadoes, and floods. And I know that you are. But, Lord, I have some powerful storms in my life right now that have nothing to do with the weather. I sometimes feel like I'm in a little boat in the middle of the ocean. I'm afraid what's going on in my life is going to drown me in sadness or anger or fear.

Help me to remember, Lord, that you have just as much power over the storms in my life as you had over that storm on the Sea of Galilee when you were in that little boat. Help me to have faith that you will take care of me—even when the storms rage so hard I feel lost and alone. Thank you for your strength over my storms, Lord.

The Lord doesn't always stop the winds from blowing in our lives, but he does take hold of our hands and lead us through the storms.

September 26

Consider it pure joy, my brothers, whenever you face
trials of many kinds, because you know that the
testing of your faith develops perseverance...so
that you may be mature and complete.

James 1:2–4, NIV

Father,

It's only been a month or so, and I'm already so tired
of school I almost can't stand it. I want to just skip it and
move on to the next part of my life. So much of it is boring. And I've got to put up with all of the teachers and
assignments and gym class. It's not all bad, but it gets so
old after a while.

You know, Father, I don't always feel this way—just
sometimes. Help me to have the right attitude about
school. Please give me the patience to get through each
class and each day. Please give me some kind of vision as
to why I'm doing this. Please help me, while I'm there, to
use my time wisely and to encourage the people you put
in my life.

*School isn't just about learning what's in
the books; it's also about learning to
depend on God in all kinds of situations.*

September 27

And this same God who takes care of me will
supply all your needs from his glorious riches, which
have been given to us in Christ Jesus.
Philippians 4:19, NLT

God,

I love you, and I need you. For some reason, it's easy
for me to forget that I need you. I get caught up in life—
school, friends, family, sports, church. I start coasting,
especially when I'm feeling good about the way things are
going. I seem to think that it's all me making things happen, keeping life on track.

Help me to remember that I still need you, that it's you
who is watching out for me. You're the one meeting my
needs and giving me good gifts. Thank you for that, Father.
Thank you that you love me and take care of me, even
when I take you for granted.

I hope you know that I do realize I always need you.

*None of us ever understand how much we need God. He
created the air we breathe and the ground we stand on. He
holds the universe together, and he's involved in every moment
of our lives. Without him, there is no us.*

He who builds his lofty palace in the
heavens and sets its foundation on the
earth, who calls for the waters of the
sea and pours them out over the face of
the land—the Lord is his name.

Amos 9:6, NIV

Move our hearts with the calm, smooth flow
of your grace. Let the river of your love run
through our souls. May my soul be carried by
the current of your love, towards the wide, infi-
nite ocean of heaven.

Stretch out my heart with your strength, as
you stretch out the sky above the earth.
Smooth out any wrinkles of hatred or resentment. Enlarge my soul that it may know more
fully your truth.

—*Gilbert of Holyland*

*Water is always moving, always changing,
always making things new. God's grace is
like that—always bringing life, always
changing us for the better.*

That means we will not compare ourselves with
each other as if one of us were better and another
worse. We have far more interesting things to do
with our lives. Each of us is an original.
Galatians 5:26, TM

God,

I don't always feel like I'm very original. Ordinary, yes—original, no.

Some people are such free spirits—they dress the way they want; they don't care what people think about their hair (not matter how strange it is); and they certainly don't care if anyone thinks they're weird. I wish I could be that way—be myself with no fear. But I could *never* pull it off.

Most of the time, I end up doing just the opposite. I try to be like other people so that I fit in and am accepted. Instead of being happy about being an original, I do everything in my power to try and conform to the mold of the average, normal person.

God, I don't want to be so outrageously different that I make a spectacle of myself. But I also don't want to spend so much energy trying to be like everyone else. Help me find some middle ground, please. Amen.

September 30

God has made everything beautiful for its own time.
Ecclesiastes 3:11, NLT

Father,

I love the fall. I hate to see summer go (except for the humidity and the bugs), but I really like the cooler weather of autumn. Thank you for the crispness of the air and for the need to wear a jacket and for great football games to watch. I really want to enjoy this fall. Even though it's a season of ending, I want it to be a new beginning for me.

Help me, this season, Father, to honor you with the way I live my life. Help me to be an encouragement to my friends and family. Help me not to get bogged down in worrying about everything, but to enjoy my life as a gift from you. Help me to be grateful for the season and everything you bring my way for the next few months.

Each new season is a gift from God. It's a new opportunity to notice all over again the beauty of his creation and the steadiness of his love for us.

My Thoughts & Prayers

What's been on your mind (and heart) this month? Have you had any big answers to prayer? What's your most important prayer request? Use this space to keep track of all that's been going on.

_____

_____

_____

_____

_____

_____

_____

_____

_____

_____

_____

_____

_____

_____

_____

_____

_____

_____

October 1

> **Oh the depth of the riches of the wisdom and knowledge of God! How unsearchable his judgments, and his paths beyond tracing out! . . . For from him and through him and to him are all things. To him be the glory forever! Amen.**
> *Romans 11:33, 36, NIV*

God,

You are way too big for me to understand. I try to think about you existing always, without a beginning or an ending. I try to think about you creating everything in the universe. I try to think about you being everywhere at once. I try to think about you never changing—even a little—over all eternity.

All that thinking doesn't get me very far. I just want to thank you that you *are*, that you exist. And that, as huge and powerful as you are, you took that time to think about me. You—the God of the universe—care about me, one person in one little place on one small planet. It's just too much!

If the human mind could understand God, he wouldn't be God. All we can do is admit that he's beyond us and praise him.

From the time the world was created, people have seen the earth and sky and all that God made. They can clearly see his invisible qualities—his eternal power and divine nature. So they have no excuse whatsoever for not knowing God.
Romans 1:19–20, NLT

Dear Lord,

Your creation is so amazing and mysterious that I can't even think of words beautiful enough to describe it.

How did you form the mountains? How did you come up with the way-out-there idea of a platypus? Why did you make so many different kinds of trees? Why did you put so much incredible beauty under the ocean—where almost no one sees it? With all the trillions of people that have lived on earth, how is it possible that no two have ever been exactly alike? What made you create things like laughter and tears and humor and singing?

I just cannot believe how intricate and detailed and marvelous everything is. It's obvious that you're an artist, that you're creative, scientific, humorous, thoughtful, and powerful. What a great time you must have had coming up with so many ideas. Thank you for making this world such a wonderful and interesting place. Amen.

In the absence of any other proof, the thumb alone would convince me of God's existence.
—Sir Isaac Newton

October 3

Jesus looked at them and said, "For mortals it is impossible,
but not for God; for God all things are possible."
Mark 10:27, NRSV

Lord, how much juice you can squeeze from a
     single grape.
How much water you can draw from a single well.
How great a fire you can kindle from a tiny spark.
How great a tree you can grow from a tiny seed.
My soul is so dry that by itself it cannot pray;
Yet you can squeeze from it the juice of a
     thousand prayers.
My soul is so parched that by itself it cannot love;
Yet you can draw from it boundless love for you
     and for my neighbor.
My soul is so cold that by itself it has no joy;
Yet you can light the fire of heavenly joy within me.
My soul is so feeble that by itself it has no faith;
Yet by your power my faith grows to a great height.
Thank you for prayer, for love, for joy, for faith;
Let me always be prayerful, loving, joyful, faithful.
          —*Guigo the Carthusian*

*The greatest miracles are the ones that
happen inside of you—through God—as
you become more loving, more passionate,
more joyful, and more full of faith.*

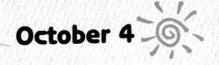

Now may our Lord Jesus Christ himself and
God our Father, who loved us and through
grace gave us eternal comfort and good hope,
comfort your hearts and strengthen them in
every good work and word.
2 Thessalonians 2:16, NRSV

Lord,

I've noticed that the way the Bible describes love is very different from how most everyone else seems to think about it. From movies and TV, you'd get the idea that love is just something that happens to you. You'd think it's a feeling that moves into your heart—and can move out just as quickly. I don't want that kind of love.

I want the kind of love you give to me, Lord. You committed yourself to me. All I had to do was say yes, and you told me we'd be together forever. I know that since then I've done things you don't like, but you're still here. You're not leaving. I want to give that kind of love to other people—especially if I get married someday. Help me learn to love as you do. Help me understand that love isn't something that happens to me, but something I choose to give.

Contrary to popular belief, love is actually a reflection of how much we "honor" another person—for at its core genuine love is a decision, not a feeling.
—Gary Smalley with John Trent, Love is a Decision

October 5

It is not an enemy who taunts me—I could bear that. It is not my foes who so arrogantly insult me—I could have hidden from them. Instead, it is you—my equal, my companion and close friend. What good fellowship we enjoyed as we walked together to the house of God.
Psalm 55:12–13, NLT

God,

I feel so alone and betrayed. One of my friends has really hurt me. I don't think anything hurts as bad as having a close friend turn against you. It's a terrible betrayal, and I don't feel like I can ever get over it.

I don't understand why my friend wanted to hurt me. I don't understand how things like this happen. One little word, one little misunderstanding, and suddenly friends are enemies. It's painful and awkward and heart-breaking and horrid. It's just plain awful.

I'm in so much pain, God. Please help me fix my broken heart. Then, please help me work to fix my broken friendship. Give me the strength to both apologize and forgive. I know it will be hard, but I want to try to save this friendship. I really cared about my friend, and I know that deep down, I still do. Amen.

**The Lord came and stood there, calling as at the
other times, "Samuel! Samuel!" Then Samuel said,
"Speak, for your servant is listening."**
1 Samuel 3:10, NIV

How often do I nod,
as if I were listening,
to words I cannot hear,
because I'm thinking about something else,
because I'm planning what I intend to say.
Yet there are those who are good listeners:
a good conversationalist listens,
a good counsellor or adviser listens,
a good doctor listens, a good judge,
a good friend.
And you, my Lord,
you listen even to my thoughts.
Teach me to listen,
that I may hear when you speak
in the wind, in music,
and in love.

—*Frank Topping*, Lord of Life

*The most important thing one friend can do for
another is to listen. Of all the friends you will
ever have, the best listener will always be God.*

**With promises like this to pull us on, dear friends,
let's make a clean break with everything that defiles
or distracts us, both within and without.**
2 Corinthians 7:1, TM

Father,

I want so much to follow you and live the right way. There are so many distractions around me, though, that sometimes it feels impossible. I can't totally hide from everything that's bad. So much of it is right there, in my face, whether I want it to be or not. How can I possibly keep from seeing some of it?

All I can do is try my best to not intentionally surround myself with those types of things. If there are certain people who drag me down, I should probably spend less time with them. If there are certain TV shows that make me think about love and life in the wrong way, I probably shouldn't watch them. There are some things that I can do to protect myself without having to totally hide under a rock. Help me recognize them, God. And then help me follow through with them.

*There's no way to deny it: What you see, what you
hear, and what you pay attention to will affect
what you believe, what you say, and how you live.*

Show me your unfailing love in wonderful ways.
You save with your strength those who seek
refuge from their enemies.
Psalm 17:7, NIV

God,
    I know this girl who doesn't seem to care about what happens to her at all. She's with a different guy every other week, and they all treat her really badly. I don't know why she puts up with that kind of treatment. I don't think she likes herself very much.
    God, I hurt for this girl. I can't help but think that maybe I would feel the same as her if I didn't know how much you love me. If I didn't have you as the perfect Father who loves me without any strings attached, I probably couldn't come up with any good reasons to like me either. Please help her to get some idea of how much you love her and want to take care of her. Please show her that love doesn't mean being treated poorly and getting hurt. Help her to find you.

Love changes everything. A person who
knows she is loved begins to see herself
with new eyes. If someone can love me,
she realizes, then I must be worth loving.
God can give that love.

Jesus said, "You have heard that the law of Moses says, 'Love your neighbor' and hate your enemy. But I say, love your enemies. Pray for those who persecute you! In that way, you will be acting as true children of your Father in heaven."

Matthew 5:43–45, NLT

Lord,

There's this group of people who always seem to be out to get me. I know I sound paranoid, but they really seem to have it in for me. I don't know why it has to be this way. I don't get it, but I want it to stop. It makes me so mad. Why can't they just leave me alone? I know it's awful, but at times I think about all of the terrible things I'd like to have happen to them.

I know that's not how you want me to think, though. You want me to love them. You want me to pray for them. It's going to be hard, but I will do that—but only for you. Please help those people figure out how much you love them. Please help them accept your love, because then I know they'd see how awful they're acting. And help me to know how to respond to them. Amen.

It's hard to stay bitter toward someone you're praying for. Praying for people makes you think about what they need—and needy people are harder to hate.

My dear brothers and sisters, be quick to listen,
slow to speak, and slow to get angry. Your anger
can never make things right in God's sight.
James 1:19–20, NLT

Lord,

Anger comes so naturally to me. I can fly into a rage without even trying. It doesn't take much at all—someone treating me unfairly, people taking something without asking, other kids mocking me, my friends taking advantage of me. I can feel it start way down in my stomach and then grow and grow until my blood seems to boil in my head. Next thing I know, my anger is controlling me and I'm saying or doing things I'll regret.

Father, help me to control my anger. Help me to remember to calm down when I feel that tightening in the pit of my stomach. Help me to turn to you about my anger sooner—at the time when I really need your help and my temper's easier to control. But if I don't turn to you quickly enough, help me to remember that I have you even when I feel my blood boiling. If I just stopped and thought of you, I know it would help. Thank you that you don't express your anger to me. Help me to follow your example and not express my full anger to others.

When angry, count ten before you speak;
if very angry, a hundred.
—Thomas Jefferson

We all make many mistakes, but those who control their tongues can also control themselves in every other way. We can make a large horse turn around and go wherever we want by means of a small bit in its mouth. And a tiny rudder makes a huge ship turn wherever the pilot wants it to go, even though the winds are strong. So also, the tongue is a small thing, but what enormous damage it can do. A tiny spark can set a great forest on fire.

James 3:2–5, NLT

God,

OK, OK, I just can't get away from how much you want me to watch my words. I mean, it's all over the place in the Bible. You talk about it over and over again. Obviously, it's important. (But that doesn't mean it's easy!)

I know how powerful words can be. I've seen the damage they can do. One little sentence spoken to only one person spreads through a crowd like a fire. And if the sentence is damaging, it doesn't take long before a few words have ruined someone's reputation. The saddest part is that most of the time, the words aren't even true.

God, I don't want to be responsible for hurting someone because of what I say. It shouldn't be so difficult to stay in control of my speech, but I think I'll struggle with it my whole life. Give me the ability to stay quiet, God, when I have nothing important to say. Make me always remember how important it is to you that I watch what I talk about. Amen.

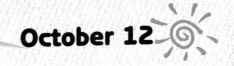

October 12

The Lord said, "Can anyone hide from me?
Am I not everywhere in all heaven and earth?"
Jeremiah 23:24, TLB

Lord, you are here,
Lord, you are there.
You are wherever we go.
Lord, you guide us,
Lord, you protect us.
You are wherever we go.
Lord, we need you,
Lord, we trust you,
You are wherever we go.
Lord, we love you,
Lord, we praise you,
You are wherever we go.
*—a daily chant of the
Dinka people*

*Wherever you go, wherever you look, wherever you
travel, wherever you tread—whether to the left or to
the right, whether up to the sky or down to the
sea—God is already there, waiting for you to arrive.*

October 13

Father,

I want money. There. I've said it—and you and I both know how true it is. You know how much I always seem to want or need something that costs more money. And I get so tired of having to watch what I spend and not do cool things because I don't have enough money. It stinks! I just want to be really, really rich. I don't want to ever have to worry about money at all.

It's so scary how much I want that. It makes me wonder what I'd be willing to do to get money. I wonder if I'd compromise what I believe. I wonder if I'd end up working so much that I miss out on other things. I wonder if I'd end up loving money more than you. I guess knowing that's a weakness is a good thing. Father, help me to always keep that weakness in mind. Help me to never put my desire for money ahead of more important things—like you.

How we use our money demonstrates the reality of our love for God. . . . The use of possessions shows us up for what we actually are.

—Charles Ryrie

So we have stopped evaluating others by what the world thinks about them. Once I mistakenly thought of Christ that way, as though he were merely a human being. How differently I think about him now! What this means is that those who become Christians become new persons. They are not the same anymore, for the old life is gone. A new life has begun!

2 Corinthians 5:16–17, NLT

Jesus,

I don't understand it. I don't even have a clue about why and how you do what you do—give people a new life and a second chance. But, Lord, I'm *so* glad.

I've made plenty of mistakes in my life. I've hurt my friends. I've definitely hurt my parents. Even though the mistakes I've made seem pretty small and not that important, it means so much to me that you've given me a chance to start fresh again. It's a wonderful feeling that I can't describe: It's like I've been washed or re-created or reborn. Thank you for that. It's a beautiful feeling!

God doesn't just want to fix your life; he wants to give you the present of a whole new life.

> **But the fruit of the Spirit is love, joy, peace, patience, kindness, goodness, faithfulness, gentleness and self-control. Against such things there is no law.**
> *Galatians, 5:22–23, NIV*

Jesus,

There are a few people in my life who seem so peaceful and content. OK, they don't live very glamorous lives. I mean, they don't own a lot of expensive things and their lifestyles aren't really fancy. They're just...well, it's hard to put into words, but they seem so relaxed and happy with life.

I want to be that way when I get older. I want others to see in me a kind of joy and contentment that can only come from you. I want not to be worried about material things or what the world defines as "success." I don't want to be a slave to my job. I want to enjoy and appreciate my life instead of always wishing it were somehow better. I know the only way my life can ever get better is through you, not through things or money or fame.

Help me develop a character that is balanced and settled and controlled. Amen.

Living a balanced life is much more fulfilling than living a glamorous life. Glamour fades easily, while a sense of balance just keeps getting stronger and stronger.

Truth, righteousness, peace, faith, and salvation
are more than words. Learn how to apply them.
You'll need them throughout your life.
Ephesians 6:14–17, TM

Dear God,
    My faith in you is very real. I know that we have a relationship that will last forever. But I don't always know what that means for my everyday life. I can't exactly walk around with a sign that advertises what I believe.
    So how am I supposed to make my everyday life about you? I want to learn more about living for you. I want the things I know to be more than words—I want them to be part of my life. Help me to understand how to live truthfully, how to live peacefully, and how to make my faith central to everything I do. If I'm going to believe in you, I want to do it with all of my energy for every day of the rest of my life.

God is not a person you can love half-
heartedly, follow just some of the time,
or believe in with only part of your mind.
He wants it all.

October 17

> But you desire honesty from the heart, so you
> can teach me to be wise in my inmost being.
> *Psalm 51:6, NLT*

Lord,

I want to be honest with you about everything. But I know that starts with being honest with myself. And sometimes that's not easy. It's easier to just coast through life and not evaluate what I'm doing or feeling, not think about what's wrong or what's right.

I don't like to admit to myself that I like to do what's wrong sometimes. I don't like to admit to myself that I feel negative emotions like anger or sadness or fear. I don't like to admit to myself when I feel jealous or envious. But if I can't be honest with myself about these things, then I can't deal with them, and I can't talk to you about them.

Help me to tell myself the truth, Lord.

If you can't tell yourself the truth, you'll never be able to be completely honest with anyone else—including God.

October 18

> But we have this treasure in jars of
> clay to show that this all-surpassing
> power is from God and not from us.
> *2 Corinthians 4:7, NIV*

God,

I think about your power a lot. It's awesome. You created a whole universe in six days. You separated a sea so your people could cross to safety. You sent your son to earth as a man and God at the same time. And after you sacrificed him for our sins, you had the power to turn death back into life.

Obviously, God, compared to you, I'm not powerful at all. I can't raise the dead. I can't create life. Still, you put your power—your spirit—in me when I became your child. I almost can't believe that, but I don't know how else to explain this ability I have to live for you. It must be your power, because I know it's not mine.

Thank you, God, for your power in me.

October 19

But the Counselor, the Holy Spirit, whom the Father will send
in my name, will teach you all things and will remind you of
everything I have said to you.

John 14:26, NIV

May your Spirit guide my mind,
Which is so often dull and empty.
Let my thoughts always be on you,
And let me see you in all things.

May your Spirit quicken my soul,
Which is so often listless and lethargic.
Let my soul be awake to your presence,
And let me know you in all things.

May your Spirit melt my heart,
Which is so often cold and indifferent.
Let my heart be warmed by your love,
And let me feel you in all things.

—Johann Freylinghausen, Spiritual Songbook

*Just as the fluid in the eye keeps the dirt out of the eyes, so
the constant cleansing of the Holy Spirit will keep the filth of
the world out of the heart.*

—Myron Boyd

Fear of the Lord is the beginning of knowledge.
Only fools despise wisdom and discipline.
Proverbs 1:7, NLT

Dear God,
   Help! I think my brain's going to explode! There are so many things to remember. School can get so hard with the quizzes and papers and tests and projects. Some days, I'm not sure I can fit it all into my head! And the worst part is that what seems so easy for some of my friends can be really tough for me.
   God, I know you've given me a mind so I can learn. You've put me in a place where I can get an education. Please help me to do that. Help me focus and concentrate when I'm in class. Help me remember all that stuff I read and study. Help me not to be so proud that I don't ask the teacher for help if I need it. And please help me not to give up, because I really want to sometimes.

All true knowledge is God's
knowledge, and that
makes it worth knowing.

October 21

It is impossible for God to lie.
Hebrews 6:18, NLT

My Lord,

I always have to think carefully about what other people tell me. I have to wonder if I can trust them. I have to ask myself if they're telling me the truth. If something comes over the Web or the TV, then I know to be careful. I've been lied to a lot from those places. If it's a friend who's told me lies before, I always think hard about what he or she is saying to make sure I'm not being deceived.

But God, I don't ever feel like I have to be careful about what you tell me in the Bible. You've never lied to me about anything—why would you start now? You're completely trustworthy in every way. You are the standard. Period. What a relief to not ever have to second-guess you! Thanks for always telling me the truth.

What would be the point of a God you couldn't trust?

"In your anger do not sin.": Do not let the sun go down while you are still angry, and do not give the devil a foothold.
Ephesians 4:26–27, NIV

Father,

I can get so angry. Sometimes I spend hours just thinking about something that made me mad, telling that person off in my head. I try to let it go, but it keeps eating at me, coming back into my thoughts. It's like I'm obsessed. I don't like my anger to control me like that.

God, I want you to help me to let go of my anger when it comes. When I get like that, I don't think very well. I tend to do things I later regret. Help me to stay under control, to be honest with you about my anger, and to trust you to handle the situation. I don't want to be known as an angry person.

Anger is a wind which blows out the lamp of the mind.
—Anonymous

I no longer call you servants, because a servant does not know his master's business. Instead, I have called you friends, for everything that I learned from my Father I have made known to you.

John 15:15, NIV

Jesus Christ, the love that gives love,
You are higher than the highest star;
You are deeper than the deepest sea;
You cherish us as your own family;
You embrace us as your own spouse;
You rule over us as your own subjects;
you welcome us as your dearest friend.
Let all the world worship you.

—Hildegard of Bingen

Jesus calls us his brothers, sisters, sheep, heirs, co-laborers, children . . . but most of all, he calls us his friends.

Father,

All of the good stuff in my life seems to be *way* out there in the future somewhere. Graduation. Freedom. College. Money. Marriage. Career. Kids. My current life is all about getting ready for that stuff. Frankly, I'm getting tired of the waiting. I want my life to start now, not later.

Help me to be patient and to wait on your timing. I know in my head that your timing is always best, but it sure feels slow to me these days. Thank you that both my right-now and my future are in your hands. Help me to be well prepared for whatever you'll bring my way. And help me not to get bored and run ahead of you. Amen.

Waiting on God isn't the same as waiting for a bus that's late or for your friend to call. You're not really waiting on him; you're only waiting for the time to be just right. He always knows the perfect time for everything, and he's never late.

> And they took offense at him. But Jesus said to them, "Only in his hometown and in his own house is a prophet without honor."
>
> **Matthew 13:57, NIV**

Jesus,

The people in your hometown saw how wise you were. They saw your miracles. And they still got offended by you. They knew you. They knew your earthly family. They had watched you grow up. I don't get why it bothered them to see you acting like the Son of God. What was the problem?

Actually, I can kind of understand a little. I sometimes feel like my family and friends don't expect me to change and grow, either. They seem to want me to fit into the same little box I've always been in. When I find a new interest or develop new attitudes, it's like they think I'm rejecting them. I guess you know how I feel.

Help me to love these people, but help me to keep growing into the person you want me to be, Lord.

October 26

Do not worship any other gods besides me.
Exodus 20:3, NLT

Lord,

I love to win, and I hate to lose. I'm sure you're not surprised by this, but sometimes my competitiveness takes over. During a game or even a whole season, I can get so focused that nothing else matters—including people who are important to me. And when I lose, I get so depressed and angry that those people don't want to be anywhere near me.

Lord, I enjoy competing, but help me to keep it in perspective. Help me not to get so caught up in winning and my performance that nothing else matters. And help me to be able to let go when a game is over. I do want to honor you by doing well, Lord, but I don't want this desire to win to take your place in my heart or to make me unbearable to others.

The need to win can become like a god that demands all your time, attention, and energy—and sucks all the joy out of playing.

October 27

And since you know that he cares, let your language show it.
Don't add words like, "I swear to God" to your own words.
Don't show your impatience by concocting oaths to hurry up
God. Just say yes or no. Just say what is true. That way, your
language can't be used against you.

James 5:12, TM

Lord God,
I think it's funny when people who don't believe in you use your name as a way to give their promises more meaning. Your name has value, even for people who don't honor it.

It's easy for me to do the same when I make a promise. I don't use your name, but I try to make my word more trustworthy by dressing it up in all kinds of extra promises and flowery words. What a waste of breath! If a person can't be trusted to follow through on their "yes," then extra words certainly aren't going to help any, are they?

I want to be a person who is known to speak the truth and to follow through on what I say. That would be one of the greatest things I could ever accomplish. Amen.

If anyone speaks, he should do it as one
speaking the very words of God. If anyone
serves, he should do it with the strength God
provides, so that in all things God may be
praised through Jesus Christ. To him be the
glory and the power for ever and ever. Amen.

1 Peter 4:11, NIV

O God, early in the morning I cry to you.
Help me to pray, and to think only of you.
I cannot pray alone.

In me there is darkness,
But with you there is light;
I am lonely, but you never leave me;
I am feeble in heart, but you are always strong.
I am restless, but in you there is peace.
In me there is bitterness, but with you patience;
I do not understand your ways,
But you know the way for me. . . .

—Dietrich Bonhoeffer

Jesus said, "Do not store up for yourselves treasures on earth, where moth and rust destroy, and where thieves break in and steal. But store up for yourselves treasures in heaven, where moth and rust do not destroy and where thieves do not break in and steal. For where your treasure is, there your heart will be also."

Matthew 6:19–21, NIV

Lord,

I want so many things—and they all cost money. Some of the things I want are to replace this old stuff I have. Other things I just want. A car. A really fast computer. Clothes. A great stereo. CDs. Stuff for my room. Cool shoes. Games. Sometimes I want that stuff so much it's all I think about, and I don't have even close to enough money to buy most of it.

Why is getting things so important to me? I want to pray that you'll give me everything I want—but I've got a hunch that won't happen. So help me to be content with what you do give me. Help me to be thankful. And help me to care more about my relationships with you and heaven and friends and family than I do about all that (really cool) stuff.

The lie of materialism is that the next new thing will satisfy you. But it doesn't work that way; there's always one more next new thing out there to covet.

> Your unfailing love, O Lord, is as vast as the heavens; your faithfulness reaches beyond the clouds. Your righteousness is like the mighty mountains, your justice like the ocean depths. You care for people and animals alike, O Lord. How precious is your unfailing love, O God!
>
> **Psalm 36:5–6, NLT**

God, I'm here. Can you see me? I'm alive. Can you feel me? I'm speaking. Can you hear me? I'm breathing. Can you sense me?

You are awesome. You are magnificent. You are mighty. You are so far beyond anything I've ever known or experienced.

And I'm just me. Just a person. Just a somebody. Just one single human being in your world full of beauty, majesty, splendor, and wonder.

It takes my breath away to think that you love me. Always. Forever. No matter what. No matter when. No matter where. It's almost too much for me to comprehend. Thank you, God, and I love you, too!

God can mean everything to you— if you allow him. You mean everything to him—no matter what.

October 31

Always be prepared to give an answer to everyone who asks you to give the reason for the hope that you have. But do this with gentleness and respect.
1 Peter 3:15, NIV

God,

   Halloween is all about masks and pretending. And that's great for fun, but I want people to see the true me in real life. I want people to see something different in me. I know you've changed me. You've given me heaven to look forward to and your spirit to guide me through this life. You've made me a new person. I don't want any masks that I'm mistakenly wearing or that other people have put on me to hide that. I want people at school and at work and in my family to see the difference you've made so they'll know how powerful you are.

   I think I must get in the way of letting them see you in me sometimes. Please help me to remove those masks from my spiritual face. Give me the motivation and the energy to live this life in a way that shines out the truth. And when people do notice, help me know what to say to them about you. Amen.

"What would Jesus do?" is more than just a catchphrase. Imagine how this world would change if every person who claims to follow Jesus actually lived and loved as he did.

My Thoughts & Prayers

What's been on your mind (and heart) this month? Have you had any big answers to prayer? What's your most important prayer request? Use this space to keep track of all that's been going on.

_____

_____

_____

_____

_____

_____

_____

_____

_____

_____

_____

_____

_____

_____

_____

_____

_____

_____

You have heard that the law of Moses says, "If an eye is injured, injure the eye of the person who did it. If a tooth gets knocked out, knock out the tooth of the person who did it." But I say, don't resist an evil person! If you are slapped on the right cheek, turn the other, too.

Matthew 5:38–39, NLT

Jesus,

You said some hard things while you were living as a human on the earth. Don't resist an evil person? Let him hit me—twice? Wow. You know that doesn't come naturally to me. I'm all about standing up for myself and fighting for my rights and not letting anyone take advantage of me.

But I guess if you'd had the same attitude, you would never have gone to the cross. And what a loss that would've been! Still, if you want me to live that way, you're going to have to help me. Please give me the wisdom to know what it means to follow your teachings—and the courage to try to do it.

Jesus always practiced what he preached. Non-resistance is the ultimate act of trust in God. For Jesus, it was also an act of love for us.

**Don't worry about the wicked. Don't envy those
who do wrong. For like grass, they soon fade
away. Like springtime flowers, they soon wither.**
Psalm 37:1–2, NLT

God, sometimes it feels like the guys in the black hats
are doing all the winning down here. They're the most popular; they have the coolest cars; they have tons of money;
and even the teachers love them. But they treat people
who aren't part of their crowd like they don't even exist. It
feels awful when the most popular kid in the class laughs
at you. Or—worse—ignores you.

I try to remember that I'm your child and that makes
all the rest of this stuff silly. But it's hard when I'm sitting
alone in the cafeteria, watching a whole pack of classmates
laughing and making plans for after school.

My mom says my turn will come. One day I'll be the
coolest at something important. Any chance we could
hurry that day along, Lord?

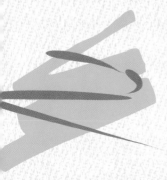

November 3

Jesus said, "Give your entire attention to what God is doing right now, and don't get worked up about what may or may not happen tomorrow. God will help you deal with whatever hard things come up when the time comes."
Matthew 6:33–34, TM

God,

    I know you don't want me to spend all my time worrying, but do you have any idea what my life is like? I have to worry about getting homework done on time. I have to worry about making decent grades. I have to worry about deciding whether I want to go to college. I have to worry about paying for college if I do decide to go. I have to worry about choosing a job. I have to worry about finding someone special to love and to love me. I have to worry that I might get some terrible disease that can't be cured. It's a lot to think about, and it drives me crazy!

    OK...I know I don't *have* to worry. But I do worry. I'd like to be more relaxed and content; I want to trust that you will take care of me and that you have a plan for my life. Please help me with that, God.

If you spend all your time worrying about the bad things that may happen, you'll miss all the good things that are happening.

Through him all things were made; without him nothing was made that has been made. In him was life, and that life was the light of men.
John 1:3–4, NIV

Father,

I've just got to praise you and thank you for this incredible universe you've created. From the tiniest little atoms circling madly inside every cell to the blue whale gliding through thousands of miles of ocean, I'm amazed when I take the time to think about what you did—and keep doing. But I don't usually take the time. I usually just plow through my days fighting to stay awake and get things done and have fun. And I spend a lot of time forgetting that you're so much bigger than any problem standing in my way.

God, help me to remember that you created all. Especially help me to remember it when I'm feeling overwhelmed by my life. You're on my side. You loved me enough to sacrifice your son. Why do I spend so much time freaking out over the small stuff?

Thanks for running the show—and for letting me watch.

November 5

All Scripture is inspired by God and is useful to teach us what is true and to make us realize what is wrong in our lives. It straightens us out and teaches us to do what is right.

2 Timothy 3:16, NLT

Dear Lord,

I want to thank you for getting your words put down in a book for me to read. When I stop to think that every time I open the Bible I'm reading God's own message to me, I'm blown away. What an incredible thing you've done to communicate with your creation.

Thank you for inspiring your people to write what you had to say. Thank you for allowing those books to be collected together to form the Bible. Thank you for protecting it through all these centuries and language changes so I could hear from you. What a great gift your words are to me. Help me not to take them for granted.

Then [Jesus] said to them all, "If any want to
become my followers, let them deny themselves
and take up their cross daily and follow me."
Luke 9:23, NRSV

In my prayers, dear Jesus, I am with you wholly.
If I meditate on the cross, I suffer with you.
If I meditate on the resurrection, I rise with you.
So daily I die and rise.

If I walk with you along the hot dusty roads,
I become hot, sweaty, tired, as you surely did.
If I hear you preach, my ears tingle with excitement,
And my heart is pierced by the sharpness of your words.
If I watch you heal people, I can feel your touch,
So my own body trembles at your power.

Let me walk with you during every minute of my life,
Let me constantly be inspired by your words,
Let me daily be renewed by your power,
That I may die to sin and rise to perfect righteousness.

—*Gemma Galgani*

November 7

> Why are you downcast, O my soul? Why so
> disturbed within me? Put your hope in God, for I
> will yet praise him, my Savior and my God.
> **Psalm 43:5, NIV**

God,

 I can't believe I got dumped. It's been a while now, but it still hurts. What's so wrong with me? I did everything I was supposed to. I said the right things. I was always there. Why should I get dumped? I don't get it.

 Help me to get past this, Father. I know it happened for a reason. I can even kind of understand why that relationship wasn't the best in the world for me. But I don't like being rejected. Help me to feel better. Help me to make a better choice next time. And help me to care more about knowing that you will always love me than I do about the fact that this one person doesn't.

Rejection always hurts. But sometimes it's the thing that pushes us in the right direction.

Consider it a sheer gift, friends, when tests and challenges come at you from all sides. You know that under pressure, your faith-life is forced into the open and shows its true colors. So don't try to get out of anything prematurely. Let it do its work so you become mature and well-developed, not deficient in any way.

James 1:2–4, TM

Father,

I know I can't expect this life to be easy, but some of the bad things that have happened to me and other people have caught me totally by surprise. I never expected to have to deal with such heavy stuff. I guess part of me thought that because I was your child, I would just kind of coast through life. I guess not.

I don't like bad things like that, Father, but I've noticed something strange. When times get really tough, I get even closer to you. I lean on you harder—and understand better that it's not possible to lean on you too hard. You're a rock. Thank you for being there during the hard times, even though I don't know why they happen. Help me to keep leaning on you instead of running away.

**Before the mountains were born
or you brought forth the earth and the world,
from everlasting to everlasting, you are God.**

Psalm 90:2, NIV

Let nothing disturb you.
Let nothing frighten you.
Everything passes.
God never changes.
Patience wins out over all.
To him who has God
Nothing is lacking.
God alone satisfies.

—St. Teresa of Ávila

*To live a steadfast and solid life,
one must have a steadfast and
solid foundation. Let God give
you that foundation.*

November 10

To the King of the ages, immortal,
invisible, the only God, be honor and
glory forever and ever. Amen.
1 Timothy 1:17, NRSV

Father,

I get so nervous before any kind of competition. My stomach gets upset, and I get distracted and can't think straight. All I can do is go over and over what I'm supposed to do and what I don't want to mess up on. Once I get going, I'm OK. But until then, I'm a complete wreck.

Father, I do ask that you'll help me to perform well, like I know I can and have done before. I ask that you'll help keep my nerves from getting in the way of my performance—or living the rest of my life. Most of all, I ask that you'll help me to honor you in my playing and to be encouraging to everyone else who's there. Thanks for the ability and opportunities you've given me.

November 11

**In everything do to others as you
would have them do to you; for this is
the law and the prophets.**
Matthew 7:12, NRSV

Dear God,

I've heard about your Golden Rule: Think of what others need and then treat them the way you'd want them to treat you. I need help with that, God, because it doesn't come naturally to me. My first thought is always, "What's best for me? What will meet my needs?"

I need to learn to think of what others might want or need, too. Please change the way I think and help me to want to help others. Then remind me to look at things from their point of view before I do something selfish.

You truly follow the Golden Rule, God. Thank you for treating me that way. You're the greatest.

*It's pretty hard to ignore
other people's needs if
you take a moment to try
to look through their eyes.*

Everyone must submit . . . to the governing authorities,
for there is no authority except that which God has
established. The authorities that exist have been
established by God.

Romans 13:1, NIV

Father,

OK, so I'm not always the best about dealing with people of authority. I admit it. But it's hard having people tell
you what to do all the time. There are always teachers,
coaches, and administrators breathing down my neck. Not
to mention my parents! Sometimes it seems like they're all
out to get me, and they don't treat me fairly. Other people
get away with so much more than I do. I wonder why you
put these authorities in my life.

Father, please give me wisdom to know how to
respond to these people. Help me to learn what I need to
from them. Give me the right attitude toward them, and
help them to see Jesus in me. And, if you will, help them
to be nicer to me, too. Thanks.

*Sometimes God puts difficult people in
our lives to change us. Sometimes he
puts us in their lives to change them.*

November 13

By the seventh day God had finished the
work he had been doing; so on the seventh
day he rested from all his work.

Genesis 2:2, NIV

Father,

Lately, it seems like I'm just going all the time. There's always something—a paper or test or assignment or practice or work or chores. Even hanging out with my friends can feel like just another thing I have to fit in. There's less and less time for sleep or relaxing. I don't know how much longer I can handle all of this rushing.

I want to rest. I want to stop and take it easy for a bit. I want to quit running so fast. Help me to know how to slow down, God. Help me to put on the brakes and live in a way that makes sense. Even you found time to rest. Help me to be like you.

Life won't leave you behind if you stop and rest. The work will wait. True rest brings the energy to keep going and the wisdom to keep going in a way that makes sense.

> The Lord is not slow in keeping his promise, as some
> understand slowness. He is patient with you, not wanting
> anyone to perish, but everyone to come to repentance.
>
> *2 Peter 3:9, NIV*

Father,

    You know how hard it is for me to start a big project. I put it off until the last possible minute, which means I have to kind of rush through it to get it done on time. It's not so bad once I'm into it; I just don't like starting. It's really kind of silly what I'll do just to avoid starting big stuff like that.

    Thank you that you're not that way. You started everything. You keep everything going. And you're going to finish everything right on your schedule. You don't procrastinate. Thank you for being so faithful and having such perfect timing. Help me to be more like you and less like me—starting right now.

Few things are as powerful as right now.

November 15

As a deer pants for water, so I long for you, O God.
Psalm 42:1, TLB

Father,

I know from the Bible that I was created to be with you. I wish I could have walked with you in the garden like Adam and Eve did. I long to be with you like that. It always feels like there's this distance between us. I know your spirit is with me, but it's just not the same as being with you face-to-face.

Father, thank you that someday I will be with you forever and ever. Thank you that this longing in my soul won't go unsatisfied. Please help me be content and at peace until that day comes. I want to live a good life here on earth with you at my side and then I want to be with you forever in heaven.

What a huge loss for Adam and Eve when they had to leave the presence of God. What a huge joy it will be when we're finally with him again in heaven.

Taste and see that the Lord is
good; blessed is the man who
takes refuge in him.
Psalm 34:8, NIV

Lord,
I need a place to hide. I need somewhere to run. My world seems to turn against me sometimes, and I feel so alone and lost. Can I just be with you awhile and not worry about anything? Can you just hold me and let me forget about all the people and situations and decisions that make me feel sad and desperate?

I need you, Lord. When I'm alone with you, I feel comforted and protected. Maybe it's because I know you accept me exactly as I am. I know I don't have to say just the right thing or be someone I'm not. You love me. You want to be with me. And I want to be with you.

Thanks for letting me hide in you.

There's nothing wrong with hiding from the world with God for a while. He loves to protect us and let us rest; then he rebuilds our strength so we can go on.

*May the God of hope fill you with all joy and peace
as you trust in him, so that you may overflow with
hope by the power of the Holy Spirit.*
Romans 15:13, NIV

Dear God,

You know my friend is hurting. Please give me wisdom and compassion so that I can help—so that I can be your soothing voice, your helpful hand, your comforting hug. Make me a good listener and a better friend than I've been.

Life can be tough when you're a teenager. There are times when nothing goes right. And when those times start coming at you again and again, start overlapping, and finally seem like a permanent way of life...well, it's the pits. Since I've been there and done that, maybe I will be able to help. Please give me the right words and an open heart. Amen.

*Hope can begin with knowing that just one
other person cares that you're hurting.*

**He will cover you with his feathers, and
under his wings you will find refuge.**
Psalm 91:4, NIV

The birds have their nests and the foxes
their holes. But you were homeless, Lord
Jesus, with nowhere to rest your head. And
yet you were a hiding-place where the sinner
could flee. Today you are still such a hiding-
place, and I flee to you. I hide myself under
your wings, and your wings cover the multitude of my sins.

—*Søren Kierkegaard*

*There is no safer home than living
under the shadow of the wings of
the one who had no home.*

November 19

Now the Lord was gracious to Sarah as he had said, and the Lord did for Sarah what he had promised. Sarah became pregnant and bore a son to Abraham in his old age, at the very time God had promised him.

Genesis 21:1–2, NIV

My Lord,

Sometimes I feel like Sarah must have felt when she heard you promise that she was going to have a son. She *was* way old, great-grandma old—definitely past her baby-making years. So she did what I probably would have done; she laughed. She pictured her old, wrinkled body getting pregnant and producing a kid, and she laughed. It must have seemed impossible to her.

I've heard your promises that you're changing me. I've heard that you've created ways for me to do your work. But sometimes I look at this life of mine and I have to laugh at that idea. I can barely do my own work, let alone yours. How could I ever do what Jesus would?

But then I look at what you did for Sarah, and it makes me realize that anything is possible for you— even changing me.

It's easier to believe what God says he will do when you stop to look at what he's already done.

November 20

**Wounds from a friend are better
than kisses from an enemy!**
Proverbs 27:6, NIV

Father,

My friend told me something once that really hurt, but now I know it was true. I didn't understand then that my friend wasn't trying to hurt me but was only trying to help me see a mistake I was making. I didn't react very well then, but now I'm grateful.

Help me, Father, to be open to helpful criticism from people I trust. Help me not to be so proud that I can never hear a negative word about myself. Thank you for my friend's help in seeing myself more clearly. Help me to change that area of my life. Also, please give me the courage to tell my friend that I appreciate the help and that I'm sorry for the way I acted then.

What you want to hear isn't always what you need to hear. The truth stings, but then it changes you. A lie can feel good, but it will destroy you in the long run.

November 21

Instead, be kind to each other, tenderhearted, forgiving one
another, just as God through Christ has forgiven you.
Ephesians 4:32, NLT

There are a whole lot of people, Father, I don't want to
be nice to. They don't deserve nice; they deserve justice—
for things they've done to me, things they've done to others, hurts they've caused. Why would anyone want to be
nice to them?

You were nice to them, though. In fact, you were more
than nice to them, weren't you? You sent Jesus to die for
them. You love them. Is that as hard for you as it is for
me? I guess not. I need your help, Father, to love them like
you do. It helps to remember that Jesus died for my sins,
too—that I'm not always lovable. Help me to be kind
because you asked me to be and because you've been
kind to me.

*No one always deserves
forgiveness. It's a gift
we give because God
gave it to us.*

I give thanks to you, O Lord my God, with my whole heart, and I will glorify your name forever.
Psalm 86:12, NRSV

Mom used to call them the "magic words": Please and Thank You. Well, God, I've used "please" enough in my prayers, so today I want to try using "thank you."

Thanks for your help studying last night. Thanks for my parents who put a roof over my head and give me a place to study—and watch TV. Thanks for my friends, especially the ones who really understand me. Thanks for your Son, who makes all of the things I go through worthwhile.

I know you've kept me safe, warm, fed, clothed. I'll try not to ever take those things for granted. Thank you. And amen.

November 23

Happy are those who do not follow the advice of
the wicked, or take the path that sinners tread,
or sit in the seat of scoffers.

Psalm 1:1, NRSV

God,

I have some friends I really like, but I know they aren't a good influence on me. I've noticed that I'm starting to talk and think like they do. I know I should make new friends, but it's scary. It's so hard to find other kids who like and accept me.

Please help me to be strong enough to give up these friendships if that's what you want. Help me to be honest with myself about why I was open to their influence on me. My relationship with you is so much more important to me than being with anyone else. Help me to keep you first.

Also, help these friends to come to know you, God. They need you as much as I do.

Friendships with people who continually lead you away from God are your least valuable possessions. Throwing them away can only help you. That doesn't mean it's easy, but it does mean it's important.

And we know that in all things God works for
  the good of those who love him, who have
    been called according to his purpose.
        Romans 8:28, NIV

God,

I've seen terrible things happen to good people—your children, people who have trusted in Jesus. They get sick. They get hurt. Their parents split up. All kinds of awful stuff happens to your kids. I don't understand that. I know you don't cause those things, but why do they happen? Why do you let humans make choices that cause such pain?

I have to choose to trust that you're still running the show and that you know what you're doing—that you've got a plan that's going to help all of this make sense. That's part of this whole deal, isn't it? Believing in you even when life doesn't make sense is where faith starts, not where it ends. Help me to keep trusting you. I know you love me, and I know you're good.

The worst time to give up on
God is when life gets hard.
That's when we need him most.

November 25

In this new life, it doesn't matter if you are a Jew
or a Gentile, circumcised or uncircumcised,
barbaric, uncivilized, slave, or free. Christ is all
that matters, and he lives in all of us.
Colossians 3:11, NLT

Father,
    I don't really get racism. It seems so obvious that
if you created all people then all people are valuable to
you—and should be valuable to us, too. Why, then, do
some people hate other races? Why do they think
they're somehow better than others? I just don't get it.
    Help me not to fall into the trap of thinking I'm
better because of my skin color or some other feature
I was born with. Help me to work toward the day when
all your children are united in you. I know that if it
never happens here on earth, it will definitely happen
in heaven. But I really want it to happen here, too,
Father. Please help us with that. Amen.

> Jesus said, "There are many rooms in my Father's home, and I am going to prepare a place for you. If this were not so, I would tell you plainly. When everything is ready, I will come and get you, so that you will always be with me where I am."
>
> *John 14:2–3, NLT*

Lord,

Thank you for giving me the goal of heaven to work toward. I can't wait to see what it will be like. It's such a great reward! After all, heaven's the point of this whole relationship with you—being with you in heaven together forever. A place with no sin and no pain and no death.

Thank you, Lord, for preparing such a great future for me and the rest of your children. Thank you for making a home for us there. Please give me the patience to wait for it and the courage to keep hoping in it. Thank you, also, for loving me so much that you guaranteed me a place there through my trust in you to save me.

If you read history you will find that the Christians who did most for the present world were precisely those who thought most of the next.

—C. S. Lewis

November 27

Jesus said, "If you sinful people know how to give good gifts to your children, how much more will your heavenly Father give good gifts to those who ask him."
Matthew 7:11, NLT

Father,

I want to give thanks for having you in my life. We're closer than ever now, I think, and I don't know enough words to thank you for all that you've done for me. I ask you for *so* much, and when you give it to me, I almost don't believe it's happening. I know I shouldn't be surprised when you give me what I ask for, but I am.

God, you always meet my needs. Thank you. It makes me love you more and trust that you do hear my prayers, both big and little. You are such a great Father to me.

I'd love to see the smile on God's face when we enjoy what he's given to us as a gift. If that makes a human father smile, God must totally beam with happiness.

November 28

**So, whether you eat or drink, or whatever you do,
do everything for the glory of God.**
1 Corinthians 10:31, NRSV

God, I totally love food! I'm crazy about so much of it—chocolate, ice cream, pizza, hamburgers. Any kind of food—it's all wonderful to me.

So now that my mind is focused on food, I just wanted to thank you for it. I mean, not just for the food. The whole idea that you would create our bodies to need food and to be able to chew it and swallow it and digest it and turn it into energy is incredible.

Then, on top of that, you allow us to be able to grow and produce and buy food to eat. And you made it fun to do. You didn't make eating a chore. You didn't make it boring. You didn't make it a "have to." You made it a "want to—right now."

Thank you, God, for all the food you provide for me to eat and for the ability you've given me to really enjoy eating it.

Eating good food with a thankful heart can be a great act of worship to God. Surely, he must relish our enjoyment of his good gifts.

November 29

But I trust in you, O Lord; I say, "You are
my God." My times are in your hand.
Psalm 31:14–15, NRSV

Father,

I'm overwhelmed by what you did for me when Jesus
died on the cross and rose again. Your book makes it clear
to me that I needed to be forgiven. I know I've sinned. And
it would have taken me forever to pay for those sins
myself.

But you did it in one moment through Jesus. You
saved me. I can never thank you enough for that. I don't
know if I'll ever even understand it. But I know you're never
going to hold my sins against me now, since I've trusted in
Jesus. I know I'm your kid and I'm yours forever.

Help me to live like I belong to you. Thank you for not
holding my sins against me.

*I could never dream a dream
for my life that would come
anywhere close to the
incredible existence God
has in store for my eternity.*

It is in vain that you rise up early and go
late to rest, eating the bread of anxious
toil; for he gives sleep to his beloved.
Psalm 127:2, NRSV

As my head rests on my pillow
Let my soul rest in your mercy.

As my limbs relax on my mattress
Let my soul relax in your peace.

As my body finds warmth beneath the blankets,
Let my soul find warmth in your love.

As my mind is filled with dreams,
Let my soul be filled with visions of heaven.
—*Johann Freylinghausen*, Spiritual Songbook

*The best way to end each day is by
falling asleep in the arms of God.*

My Thoughts & Prayers

What's been on your mind (and heart) this month? Have you had any big answers to prayer? What's your most important prayer request? Use this space to keep track of all that's been going on.

_____

_____

_____

_____

_____

_____

_____

_____

_____

_____

_____

_____

_____

_____

_____

_____

December 1

Even youths will faint and be weary, and the young will fall exhausted; but those who wait for the Lord shall renew their strength, they shall mount up with wings like eagles, they shall run and not be weary, they shall walk and not faint.

Isaiah 40:30–31, NRSV

God,

I'm tired. All I want is a chance to relax, and do nothing. But it never happens. There's always one more thing to do, one more place to go, one more person to call, one more assignment to finish, one more job to complete—I hate the thought of never being able to stop doing, doing, doing and going, going, going.

It's exhausting, God, to keep up the pace that everyone expects of me. My parents want me to do my share around the house. My friends want me to be available to go out all the time. My teachers and coaches expect the best. There's not enough of me to go around.

I need to take a look at my life to see if some things could be cut off, just so I can have some peace of mind. And I need to get enough sleep to make it through another day. But the emotional strength and energy can only come from you. I know that. And I need that. Amen.

God promises to renew you and to help you soar; he does not promise to help drag you through an unmanageable and ridiculous schedule. If you're feeling tired, if you're feeling overwhelmed, turn to him—but only after you have first evaluated your life.

Surely goodness and love will follow me
all the days of my life, and I will dwell in
the house of the Lord forever.
Psalm 23:6, NIV

O Lord, support us all the day long, until
the shadows lengthen, and the evening
comes, and the busy world is hushed, and
the fever of life is over, and our work is done.
Then in thy mercy, grant us a safe lodging,
and a holy rest, and peace at the last.
    Amen.

—Book of Common Prayer

*From morning until night, from
dusk until dawn, from yesterday
until tomorrow, God is here.*

Dear God,
    I love this time of year, when I can Christmas shop, stare at store windows, look at Santa (and remember when I believed). Now I believe in you, and I know that the gifts you give are cooler than anything Santa gave me.
    Christmas is about you, but—then again—every day is about you when I'm walking with you. So, while I really love that you came into this world in such a special way, I also love this time of year with my family and friends. We take these days to celebrate together, building memories and traditions. I think we all try to get along and be kinder to each other at Christmastime.
    Please help me to have a blessed Christmas and to pass your love on to others. I want to rejoice in your spirit and in the spirit of the holidays. Amen.

December 4

**But I trust in you, O Lord; I say, "You are
my God." My times are in your hand.**
Psalm 31:14–15, NRSV

Dear Lord,
    My friend and I have been a couple for a while now.
You know who I mean. I'm worried because I'm not sure
how much longer we'll be together. Things aren't the same.
I don't even like to think about it, but I feel like maybe
we're drifting apart.
    I'm not sure what to want. I really like having a steady
relationship, but do I want it to go on forever? I don't know.
God, please help me to know what to do. Help me to trust
you with my emotions. Help me not to try to hold on to
something that's not your best for me.

*Holding on to the wrong
thing is no better than
letting go of the right thing.*

Do not be anxious about anything, but in everything, by prayer
and petition, with thanksgiving, present your requests to God.
And the peace of God, which transcends all understanding, will
guard your hearts and your minds in Christ Jesus.

Philippians 4:6–7, NIV

Father,
   You know I'm great at worrying. I might not show it to
other people, but I'm sure you don't miss it. I just think and
worry and analyze and fret. I'm a gold-medal–class worrier!
   Sometimes my worrying can pretty much turn into
obsessive thinking. I mentally go through all the possibili-
ties and what I could do and what others will do and what
might happen to me. Other times, my anxiety turns into
this need to control everything—and everyone—in my life.
   But in the end, there's not much I can really do about
a lot of things. I know I've got to trust you to handle stuff,
but that's harder than it sounds. Help me to do that, Father.
Help me to trust you. Help me to relax and let you have
control.

*Worry starts small. One test. One problem. One
issue. But if left alone, worry gobbles up one thing
after another until it's taken over your whole mind.*

December 6

Father, you know I sometimes have a hard time telling the truth. A lie can be so convenient and make life so easy. I've found that the truth really can hurt—especially when the truth is that I've messed up or done the wrong thing. But, Father, I don't like myself very much when I lie.

Please give me the strength not to take the easy way out by lying. Help me to have the courage to tell the truth even when it hurts me. I know I'll be better off in the long run—and I know it will make you happy. Thank you that you're so strong you can make me brave enough not to lie.

Lying is easy and ultimately more destructive than any physical violence. Telling the truth can be hard, but it makes life easier in the long run.

> Instantly Jesus reached out his hand and
> grabbed [Peter]. "You don't have much faith,"
> Jesus said. "Why did you doubt me?"
> **Matthew 14:31, NLT**

Jesus,

Sometimes I feel just like Peter on that night you came walking across the water toward the boat. He was afraid until he realized it was you. Then he was so excited that he wanted to walk on the water just like you were. And then he took his eyes off of you and looked at the waves and thought, "Wait a minute! I can't do this." And he started sinking.

I do all those things. You go to work on me, and the change scares me a little at first. Then I get excited about it and start letting you do really cool things in my life. Then I start looking at all the reasons I can't be like you, and I freak out. I run back to other things because I don't think I can do anything more. I start sinking.

Please, Lord, give me the faith to keep looking at you.

It takes as much faith to follow Jesus on
land as it does to walk with him on water.

December 8

God sets the lonely in families.
Psalm 68:6, NIV

Lord God,

    You've put me in the middle of this family. You and I both know it's not like everyone else's family—but it's the one I've got. I do love these people, even though we fight sometimes. I do want them to succeed and do well. Please help each of them to find your best for their lives.

    God, thank you for every member of this family. Thank you for the person you've created each of them to be. Thank you for my time with them. Thank you that we can all laugh together sometimes even when things are hard. Thank you for helping them to be (mostly) patient with me. Help me to be patient with them, too, and to love them with your love.

Your family is the first place you practice your Christianity. You learn to love those people before you truly learn to love others.

If you have any encouragement from being united with Christ, if any comfort from his love, if any fellowship with the Spirit, if any tenderness and compassion, then make my joy complete by being like-minded, having the same love, being one in spirit and purpose.

Philippians 2:2, NIV

Lord Jesus,
help us to be more loving in our homes.
Make us thoughtful for others
and help us to think of kind things to do.
Keep us from grumbling and ill-temper
and help us to be cheerful when things go wrong
and our plans are upset.
May we learn to love
and understand each other
and think of others before ourselves.

—*Graham Salmon,* Prayers for Children and Young People

The easiest person to think of is yourself. The hardest person to think of is the other guy. It's tough, but always try to think of the other guy.

December 10

Thank you, thank you, thank you for the up-coming holiday break from school. I really need it during this time of year. I'll still have to do some reading for school and maybe write a paper, but mostly my time is my own. Maybe I can go to a movie matinee or work out at the gym. Let's face it, sleeping in is good, too.

If I can work for a few hours—babysitting, even—I could save money for something awesome. Is there something you'd like me to do? Put in some time at the soup kitchen or help my mom with something?

Before I know it the break will be over, but I plan to make good use of the time. Nudge me where you want me to go, and please watch over me while I sleep or work or hang with my friends. Amen.

December 11

Be silent, and know that I am God!
Psalm 46:10, NLT

Lord,
    My world is full of so much noise and activity. TV. Computer. Radio. I've always got some kind of information coming at me. Pictures. Magazines. Music. Ads. Games. Sometimes, it's like I'm afraid for it to be quiet or like I'm afraid to sit still.

    I've got school, sports, work, family stuff, church. I'm always going. I'm always listening to something. I'm always taking something in—right up until the minute my head hits the pillow at night.

    Help me to stop once in a while and just remember that you are God. Help me not to run from the silence, not to be afraid to be alone with you. Help me to honor you with my full attention.

Sometimes in the quiet,
God speaks the loudest.

December 12

How can a young person stay pure?
By obeying your word and following its rules.
Psalm 119:9, NLT

Father,

    Purity isn't a word that comes up much in my society. I try to stay pure of mind, body, and spirit, but most of the people on TV or in movies (and even some of my friends) seem to think that not being willing to try anything—even things that I know are wrong—is wimpy or prudish. It's hard not to give in just to get it over with.

    But, Father, I want you to be happy with what I do with my life—and my body. You know I'm going to need help with that, because I'm not strong enough on my own to live a pure life. Please keep reminding me that obeying you is worth what I'm giving up. Please give me the courage not to do what I want to do sometimes. Thank you for the times you've already helped me with that.

Like everything worth having, purity costs a lot. You might have to sacrifice certain friends, good times, opportunities. The gains of following God's path, however, far outweigh any losses.

Then Jesus said, "Come to me, all of you who are weary and carry heavy burdens, and I will give you rest. Take my yoke upon you. Let me teach you, because I am humble and gentle, and you will find rest for your souls. For my yoke fits perfectly, and the burden I give you is light."

Matthew 11:28–30, NLT

Lord,

I get so tired sometimes. So much is going on in my life, and I'm working to keep up with it all and to keep doing the right things and being kind to people and getting decent grades and being everything everyone expects me to be. It's too much! I can't keep up the pace.

Help me to do only what you want me to do. Help me to rest in you and let you do the things I can't do. Help me to trust you with the stuff that gets by me. Help me to get good sleep and keep focused on you instead of myself. Thank you.

When life gets too heavy, I sometimes realize I'm carrying way more than anyone—including God—has asked me to. When I give most of it back to him to carry, life gets much easier.

December 14

> The steps of the godly are directed by the Lord.
> He delights in every detail of their lives. Though
> they stumble, they will not fall, for the Lord
> holds them by the hand.
> **Psalm 37:23–24 , NLT**

I wish life were easier. I wish I didn't make so many mistakes. I wish I were perfect. I wish I didn't have so many struggles. I wish, I wish, I wish. . . . God, it's hard to feel good about myself when life gets rough, and I don't succeed at everything.

I wish that people who follow you never had to deal with failure and disappointment. But the Bible says I will. "Though they stumble" it says. Not "*if* they stumble" or "*just in case* they stumble" or "*maybe* they'll stumble." Since you said life would be this way, I can't get so down on myself when mistakes happen. Instead, I should just hang on to you a little tighter so that I can get back up again and keep going. Thank you for accepting me, even when I stumble. Amen.

It is not the person who stumbles who is a failure, but rather the person who refuses to get up and try again.

**Love each other with genuine affection,
and take delight in honoring each other.**
Romans 12:10, NLT

God,
  Lately, I've realized how much time I spend thinking about me. Are my clothes OK? Is my hair right? Does my breath stink? If I'm with anyone besides my family, I get *so* self-conscious. When people are talking, it's like I'm only thinking about what I'll say next. It's so weird—I want so much for other people to like me that I wind up thinking just about me and nothing about them. I become focused more on myself than on anyone else.
  Help me to start thinking about other people. Help me to trust you with how I look and what I say. Help me to be so unaware of myself that I'm free to work on being encouraging to others. Help me to be a better listener than I am a talker. Thanks, God.

***People will always appreciate
kindness and attention more
than they'll appreciate
perfection.***

December 16

For wherever there is jealousy and
selfish ambition, there you will find
disorder and every kind of evil.
James 3:16, NIV

Dear God,
     Why did the one person I could see myself
with have to end up with my good friend? It's
not fair. My friend always seems to get the
best of everything. Why can't my life be like
that? Why does my life have to be so stupid?
     I need your help, God. I know my jealousy
doesn't make you happy. And that's exactly
what it is. Jealousy. I want my friend's life. I
want my friend's relationship with that person!
Help me to get my mind off of that, Lord. Help
me to remember all the good things you've
given to me instead of thinking about what
could have been. Help me to keep thanking
you. Amen.

**For we are what he has made us, created in
Christ Jesus for good works, which God
prepared beforehand to be our way of life.**
Ephesians 2:10, NRSV

Father,
    I know you've got things for me to do. I know
you created me for a reason. I just wanted you to
know—I'm ready. Send me out there, Father. Start
me on something. I'm ready to go and do for you. I
don't want to keep sitting on the sidelines. I feel
like my time has come.
    I'm not too picky, either, Lord, about what I'll
do. I know you've created me and designed me for
something. Whatever it is, just let me know, and I'll
go do it. I'm excited about the idea of serving you
by actually doing something. Help me not to miss
what that is. Help me to do it really well, especially
since it's for you.

*Serving God as we were created
to is the most intense, thrilling,
passionate activity on earth.*

December 18

Make sure they are well versed in every branch of learning, are gifted with knowledge and good sense, and have the poise needed to serve in the royal palace.
Daniel 1:4, NLT

Lord God,
    I'm going to be honest. I don't love school. Some days I don't even like it—not even a little. And some days, I just hate it. It gets so stressful—all the papers, tests, homework, projects. When it all starts piling up, I feel like I'm drowning under the work. But I know it's important to work hard. I'll never have perfect grades, but I at least want to know I've done my best. And I don't mean that just about my grades. I want to do my best to actually *learn*. I want to learn about my subjects, and I want to learn about common sense, respect, and integrity. I'm going to study, God, but I'm also going to watch and learn. Amen.

Being wise is not just about good grades. It's about good living.

> **And without faith it is impossible to please God, because anyone who comes to him must believe that he exists and that he rewards those who earnestly seek him.**
> Hebrews 11:6, NIV

Father,

I want to thank you for making my faith in you stronger and stronger. I'm completely convinced of your existence and your love for me. I don't think I could have come this far in my belief without your help, though. I couldn't believe like this on my own.

I'm thinking of some of my family and friends who don't have faith in you. Father, I ask that you would bring them to a point of believing in you. I want them to have a relationship with you like I do. I want them to feel this kind of happiness, this kind of love. I hope they get a chance to know how peaceful and meaningful this is. Help them to trust in you.

Believing in God makes him happy. What an amazing thought—tiny humans can make their creator happy just by believing in him.

December 20

*I pray that you ... may have power ... to grasp how wide
and long and high and deep is the love of Christ, and to
know this love that surpasses knowledge.*
Ephesians 3:17–19, NIV

Lord,

Why did you do it? Why did you leave behind heaven
to come and live on this harsh planet for more than
30 years? You created every person. Why did you let some
of them talk to you so badly? Why did you work so hard to
teach your truths to those disciples? Why did you let yourself be killed?

I know the answer—love—but I don't understand that
kind of love. You could have stopped the whole thing any
time you wanted. You could have said no. But you
didn't. I don't get it, but thank you, Lord, for loving me
enough to go through all that. Thank you for my salvation.

*Nothing could have held the son of God on that
cross—except his love for us and his father.*

Ever since I heard of your strong faith in the
Lord Jesus and your love for Christians
everywhere, I have never stopped thanking
God for you. I pray for you constantly.
Ephesians 1:15–16, NLT

Dear God,

So many of your people have been good to me. Some of them I didn't even really know. But if they hadn't listened to you and accepted your Son and shared him with me through their words and their actions, if they hadn't lived for you, then I might still be lost. But because they loved and obeyed you, I've learned how to be with you forever.

God, please encourage each of your children. Let them know what a difference they're making just by doing what you've asked them and loving you back. Help them not to get discouraged, but to keep working for you. Thanks again for all of them, Father.

We'll never know how many lives we impact just by living our one life for God. It's God's way of spreading his love.

December 22

I will extol the Lord with all my heart.
Psalm 111:1

What can I give Him
Poor as I am;
If I were a shepherd,
I would give Him a lamb.
If I were a wise man,
I would do my part.
But what can I give Him?
I will give my heart.
—*Christina G. Rossetti*

Of all the things you could give to God, he doesn't want anything expensive, anything fancy, or anything extravagant. What he wants is your heart, the most priceless and precious gift of all.

The people who walk in darkness will see a great light—
a light that will shine on all who live in the land where death
casts its shadow. For a child is born to us, a son is given
to us. And the government will rest on his shoulders. These
will be his royal titles: Wonderful Counselor, Mighty God,
Everlasting Father, Prince of Peace.

Isaiah 9:2, 6, NIV

O God, thank you for being willing to come to
earth as a baby, to live a humble and simple life, to
give up the glory of heaven for the squalor of earth.
I cannot believe you love me that much. You truly are
my light in the darkness.

Thank you for so many things—for being with me
always, for granting me my prayers, for loving me, for
forgiving me. But at this time of year, I have to thank
you most of all for giving us your Son, the Prince of
Peace.

*The wonder of Christmas is not simply that God came
to earth, but that he came to earth as a helpless,
crying baby who was born in the lowliest of places
under the gaze of the lowliest of creatures.*

December 24

The Lord said, "The virgin will be with child and
will give birth to a son, and they will call him
Immanuel—which means, 'God with us.'"
Matthew 1:23, NIV

Loving Father, help us remember the birth of Jesus,
that we may share in the song of the angels, the gladness
of the shepherds, and the wisdom of the wise men.

Close the door of hate and open the door of love all
over the world.

Let kindness come with every gift and good desires
with every greeting.

Deliver us from evil by the blessing which Christ
brings, and teach us to be merry with clean hearts.

May the Christmas morning make us happy to be thy
children, and the Christmas evening bring us to our beds
with grateful thoughts, forgiving and forgiven, for Jesus'
sake. Amen.

—*Robert Louis Stevenson*

*Something to keep in mind during the
joyous Christmas season: Jesus did not
come to earth as a baby in order to know
human beings; he came to earth as a baby
in order that human beings could know God.*

December 25

There were shepherds living out in the fields nearby, keeping watch over their flocks at night. An angel of the Lord appeared to them, and the glory of the Lord shone around them, and they were terrified. But the angel said to them, "Do not be afraid. I bring you good news of great joy that will be for all the people. Today in the town of David a Savior has been born to you; he is Christ the Lord. This will be a sign to you: You will find a baby wrapped in cloths and lying in a manger." Suddenly a great company of the heavenly host appeared with the angel, praising God and saying, "Glory to God in the highest, and on earth peace to men on whom his favor rests." When the angels had left them and gone into heaven, the shepherds said to one another, "Let's go to Bethlehem and see this thing that has happened, which the Lord has told us about." So they hurried off and found Mary and Joseph, and the baby, who was lying in the manger. When they had seen him, they spread the word concerning what had been told them about this child, and all who heard it were amazed at what the shepherds said to them.

Luke 2:7–20, NIV

God, on this Christmas day let me remember that it is all about you—not food, not decorations, and not even giving gifts to one another. It is about *you* and only you. The Christ child. God come to earth as man. Thank you, and I love you. Amen.

December 26

After this interview the wise men went their way. Once again the star appeared to them, guiding them to Bethlehem. It went ahead of them and stopped over the place where the child was. When they saw the star, they were filled with joy! They entered the house where the child and his mother, Mary, were, and they fell down before him and worshiped him. Then they opened their treasure chests and gave him gifts of gold, frankincense, and myrrh.

Matthew 2:9–11, NLT

Jesus,

I want to see the star the wise men followed. I want to see it so I can follow it, too. I need something to guide me and lead me to you. It's easy for me to lose sight of my way, especially in this dark world. But I'm coming. I'm on my way. And when I get there, I will do what the Magi did. I will bow down in amazement and awe because you, God, chose to live on the same earth as I. Amen.

If you saw Christ today, and he was in the form of a tiny, helpless babe, would you recognize him as the Almighty God?

Let the peace of Christ rule in your hearts,
since as members of one body you were called
to peace. And be thankful.

Colossians 3:15, NIV

This day and night,
  may I know O God
The deep peace
  of the running wave
The deep peace
  of the flowing air
The deep peace
  of the quiet earth
The deep peace
  of the shining stars
The deep peace
  of the Son of Peace.

—*J. Philip Newell*, Celtic Prayers
from Iona

*Even in chaos, Jesus gives peace to those who walk with him.
He doesn't ask us to struggle through life on our own. Instead,
he asks us to walk in his power through a difficult life.*

December 28

Before the mountains were brought forth, or ever you had formed the earth and the world, from everlasting to everlasting you are God.
Psalm 90:2, NRSV

God,

I try to understand who you are, and I feel like I'm swimming in a great, big, huge ocean; I'm a speck in a seemingly endless sea of water. You've always existed, and you will always exist. You've got no beginning, no ending. You just are. No wonder you call yourself "I Am." That's a perfect name for you.

Thank you, God, that you are eternal. Thank you that I don't need to completely comprehend what that is to make it true. I praise you for being so far beyond me, but going to all the trouble to reach out to me, to communicate to me, to explain yourself (at least as much as I can understand). You are truly amazing.

If the truth of who God is depended on our ability to understand it, he would be a much, much smaller God.

> But if you are unwilling to serve the Lord,
> then choose today whom you will serve.
> Joshua 24:15, NLT

Jesus,

I don't know if I've ever really chosen who to serve. I love and follow you, but have I ever really chosen you? Maybe that's something I need to do now—to consciously say, "I will serve you. I will not serve money. I will not serve popularity. I will not serve success. I will not serve power. I will not serve fame. I will not serve recognition. I will serve you and only you."

I truly mean that. I can't just assume that I've chosen you simply because you've always been a part of my life. If I don't keep reminding myself who I serve, I might find myself veering off onto the wrong path without realizing it.

God, I want to serve you. Totally. Forever. Amen.

December 30

Jesus said, "Ask and it will be given to you; seek and
you will find; knock and the door will be opened to you.
For everyone who asks receives; he who seeks finds;
and to him who knocks, the door will be opened."
Matthew 7:7–8, NIV

Father, I want to thank you for answering
my prayers. I've been praying more often now
for about a year, and I've noticed something. It
makes a difference. You really do hear me and
respond, don't you? I mean, I always knew that
in my head—but now I'm seeing it in my life.

Thank you for making me your child
through Jesus and caring enough about me as
my Father to listen to me. Thank you even
more for answering me. Even when you say
no, I know it's because you love me. Help me
to remember to keep coming to you like this
with my prayers.

*What could possibly make more sense than
asking for what you want from the most
powerful and loving person in the universe?
Even if he says no, at least you've taken your
request all the way to the top.*

> **But the Lord's plans stand firm forever;**
> **his intentions can never be shaken.**
> **Psalm 33:11, NLT**

Father,

The new year is coming, and I wonder where my life is going. People keep asking me what I want to be when I grow up and lots of other questions. *What college are you going to? What are you going to major in?* Is it bad, Father, that I don't know the answers to those questions yet? I mean, it just all seems so far away. How am I supposed to know all of that stuff when I haven't tried any of it?

Thank you, Father, that you're not waiting on me to figure out those answers. Thank you that you already know my future and that you're preparing me for it. Thank you that there's nothing that will happen tomorrow or next month or three years from now that will surprise you. You've got it under control. I will trust you to help me find answers to each new question.

My Thoughts & Prayers

What's been on your mind (and heart) this month? Have you had any big answers to prayer? What's your most important prayer request? Use this space to keep track of all that's been going on.

_____

_____

_____

_____

_____

_____

_____

_____

_____

_____

_____

_____

_____

_____

_____

ACKNOWLEDGMENTS

Publications International, Ltd., has made every effort to locate the owners of all copyrighted material to obtain permission to use the selections that appear in this book. Any errors or omissions are unintentional; corrections, if necessary, will be made in future editions.

January 17: Taken from *Are You Running With Me, Jesus?* by Malcolm Boyd. Holt, Rinehart, and Winston Publishing Company, copyright © 1965.

January 21: Taken from *She Said Yes* by Misty Bernall. Plough Publishing House, copyright © 1999. Used by permission.

January 27, August 25: Excerpts from *Tough Days and Talks With God* by Dean Nadasdy. Augsburg Publishing House, copyright © 1989. Used by permission.

January 28: Taken from *A Thirty-Day Experiment in Prayer* by Robert Wood. The Upper Room, copyright © 1978. Used by permission of Upper Room Books.

February 12: Taken from *New Parish Prayers* by Frank Colquhoun. Hodder and Stoughton Publishers. Used by Permission. All rights reserved.

February 16: "Psalm 89" from *Psalms/Now* by Leslie Brandt. Concordia Publishing House, copyright © 1973. Used by permission under license number 01:01-31.

March 14: A Jewish Liturgy. Printed with permission from the Central Conference of American Rabbis (CCAR).

March 31: Excerpt from *By the Water: A Collection of Prayers for Everyday* by Ellyn Sanna. Barbour Publishing Inc., Uhrichsville, Ohio. Used by permission.

May 1, August 31: Taken from *Psalms for Teens* by Eldon Weisheit. Concordia Publishing House, copyright © 1992. Used with permission under license number 01:01-31.

May 7: "Awe-full" from *Better Than Nice and Other Conventional Prayers* by Frederick Ohler. Copyright © 1989 by Frederick Ohler. Used by permission of Westminster John Know Press.

May 17: Excerpt from *Visions of a World Hungry* by Thomas G. Pettepiece. The Upper Room, copyright © 1979. Used by permission of Upper Room Books.

May 21: Excerpt from *God Loves You* by Peter Marshall. Baker Book House Company, copyright © 1967. Used by permission.

June 22: Excerpt from *Engraved on Your Heart: Living the Ten Commandments Day by Day* by Bill Hybels. Cook Communications Ministries, copyright © 2000. May not be further reproduced. All rights reserved.

July 24: From *Worship Now* by J. L. Cowie. Used with permission by St. Andrew Press/The Church of Scotland. All rights reserved.

August 20, December 27: Excerpts from *Celtic Prayers from Iona* by J. Philip Newell. Copyright © 1997. Used with permission of Paulist Press.

September 5: Taken from *Prayers for Dark People* by W.E.B. DuBois. University of Massachusetts Press, copyright © 1980. Used by permission.

October 6: Excerpt from *Lord of Life* by Frank Topping. Published by The Lutterworth Press and used with permission.

December 9: Taken from *Prayers for Children and Young People* by Graham Salmon. Hodder and Stoughton Publishers. Used by permission. All rights reserved.